The Toronto Blessing – or Is It?

Edited by
STANLEY E. PORTER
and
PHILIP J. RICHTER

DARTON·LONGMAN +TODD

First published in 1995 by
Darton, Longman and Todd Ltd
1 Spencer Court
140–142 Wandsworth High Street
London SW18 4JJ

ISBN 0–232–52130–1

A catalogue record for this book is available
from the British Library

Phototypeset by Intype, London
Printed and Bound in Great Britain by
Page Bros, Norwich

Contents

Introduction   1

1
'God is not a Gentleman!': The Sociology of the
Toronto Blessing
PHILIP J. RICHTER   5

2
Shaking the Biblical Foundations?: The Biblical
Basis for the Toronto Blessing
STANLEY E. PORTER   38

3
Risen with Healing in His Wings: An Exploration
of the Psychology of the Toronto Blessing
ROYSE MURPHY   66

4
Have We Been Here Before?: A Historian Looks at
the Toronto Blessing
JOHN KENT   86

5
The Worship of the Toronto Blessing?
WENDY J. PORTER   104

Introduction

The Toronto Blessing is sweeping significant numbers of churches in Britain and elsewhere. What began as a local phenomenon in Toronto, Canada, has become a movement that is attracting a dedicated following among a variety of people from all walks of life. It is making its presence known in churches of various types, including Anglican, Baptist, Roman Catholic and Methodist, besides a number of charismatic groups. The claim is that this is a definite and special outpouring of God's Holy Spirit for these troubled times. At least this is what those who have experienced the Toronto Blessing would have us believe. But is this the only explanation? In January 1995 the Blessing received national media coverage when it was denounced as 'an expression of mass hysteria' in the preface to the *Church of England Yearbook*. What would others untouched by the Blessing make of the falling on the floor, the making of animal noises, the quasi-drunkenness, and the uncontrollable laughter? What would a sociologist say about the people and churches involved in it and the reasons for the forms it takes? What would a theologian say about the biblical basis of this movement, and how it interprets the Bible? What would a psychiatrist say

1

about the possible psychological causes and effects of such behaviour on those who experience them and those around them? What would a church historian say about how this particular set of charismatic phenomena compares with similar kinds of phenomena that have appeared at several of the major revivals in the past? What would a professional church musician and worship leader say about the liturgical structure of services where such phenomena are present? Just such people were asked for their trained and professional analysis of the Toronto Blessing. Stanley E. Porter and Philip J. Richter have drawn together their responses in this volume.

Philip J. Richter (BA, MA, M.Phil.) is a sociologist and an ordained minister in the Methodist Church. He has served ministerial posts in the North of England, and is currently Chaplain at Southlands College and lectures in the sociology of religion in the Department of Theology and Religious Studies at the Roehampton Institute London.

Stanley E. Porter (BA, MA, MA, Ph.D.) is Professor of Theology and Head of the Department of Theology and Religious Studies at the Roehampton Institute London. He has also taught in the USA and Canada. One of his areas of research interest is interpretative questions raised by use of the Bible in contemporary Christianity.

Royse Murphy (MB, Ch.B.) is a general medical practitioner with an interest in adult and adolescent psychiatry and psychotherapy, as well as being an ordained priest in the Anglican Church. After serving in several hospital posts and training in general practice, Royse undertook two years of full-time hospital work in psychiatry, which he continues to practise.

John Kent (MA) is Emeritus Professor of Theology at the University of Bristol and an ordained minister in the Methodist Church. He is renowned as a church historian, especially of religious revivals of the past two centuries and the various forms that they take.

Wendy J. Porter (BA) is a professional musician who has been involved in music ministry in churches around the world. She specialises in creating intelligent worship through the simple and straightforward presentation of her music. Wendy is pursuing research into the philosophical and theo-logical questions surrounding the origins of current attitudes towards the use of music in the church.

1

'God is not a Gentleman!'

The Sociology of the Toronto Blessing

PHILIP J. RICHTER

'No cameras, no recorders' reads the sign on the door of a south-west London church. Not surprisingly, many of the people currently worshipping there at Sunday services and weekday meetings would not wish to be captured on film or tape. For some it would be too embarrassing and liable to serious misinterpretation. Rolling about the floor, laughing hysterically, or staggering around as if drunk are not features that would normally be associated with church-going in Britain. But, since the 'Toronto Blessing' hit these shores, these and other unusual phenomena have become common-place at a large number of churches throughout Britain and across different denominations. Although centred outside the mainstream churches, particularly within the 'House Church' or 'New Church' movement, Vineyard Churches and the older Pentecostal churches, the Toronto Blessing has also affected individual churches within the main denominations. The Toronto Blessing is being reported within the Baptist, Methodist, Salvation Army, Roman Catholic and even Anglican Church, particularly where local churches have already previously been open to Charismatic Renewal. By October

1994 it was estimated that as many as 3000 churches had been affected (Fearon 1994: 146). Perhaps the most publicised Anglican venue has been Holy Trinity Brompton (HTB) in central London. The *Church Times* reported queues two-hours long for the Sunday evening service last summer at HTB, with up to two thousand people attending (Fearon 1994: 4).

This chapter looks at the Toronto Blessing through the eyes of a sociologist. Whilst the opinions of those who have received the Blessing will be taken seriously, the intention here is to put the Blessing into a wider context using tools from the world of sociology. There is no intention to 'explain away' the phenomena. Questions as to the truth, or otherwise, of the Blessing properly lie beyond the sphere of the sociologist.

Religious experiences are categorised by sociologists into four main types: confirming, responsive, ecstatic and revelational. The latter types are least frequently found within mainstream religion. The average mainstream church-goer may from time to time have an awareness of the Divine, helping to confirm the validity of his or her beliefs. There may even be a sense that the awareness is mutual and that the Divine has responded in some way. Much less common is the ecstatic experience of intimate relationship with the Divine and the revelational experience in which the person is given messages or a commission by the Divine. The Toronto Blessing stands out from ordinary religious experience in being predominantly ecstatic, and in some cases revelational, in form.

The Form of the Blessing

The physical characteristics of the Toronto Blessing, which are treated as 'manifestations of the Holy Spirit', are many and varied. Not every feature will be found in every church affected. Typically, you might expect to find the following features:

• **Bodily weakness and falling to the ground**. After a time of what is termed 'ministry' — special prayer by the leader or members of the leadership team — the church will often resemble a surreal battlefield, with scores of people lying on the floor. Some will be lying peacefully, some will be rolling or flailing about, some will be moving their bodies rapidly and rhythmically, even erotically, some will be making judo-like chopping actions with their forearms, some will be twitching, some will be sobbing, some will be laughing hysterically. Their 'carpet experience', as its devotees sometimes euphemistically term it, begins when the person starts to sway, fall, or their legs weaken and crumple, and they drop back into the arms of strategically-placed 'catchers'. This is described by recipients as 'falling under the weight of God's glory', being 'overcome by the Spirit' so that they may 'rest in the Spirit'. Whilst they are on the floor people often report that they feel physically anaesthetised, weighted-down or, sometimes, weight*less*, unable to get up, sometimes for hours, even when they try. They are generally aware of all that is going on around them. The experience is generally pleasurable and the person will often report later that they felt as if a high-voltage electrical charge or 'light' was sweeping through their body, making them 'tingle all over'.

• **Shaking, trembling, twitching and convulsive bodily movements**. Before or after the person falls, or independently of this, their body may twitch or shake uncontrollably. Sometimes this may resemble an epileptic seizure. Indeed children from affected churches in Toronto have been sent home with notes to their parents suggesting that their children be investigated for potential epilepsy! The 'Toronto Twitch', often experienced in the stomach region, can occasionally be quite painful, and has been compared to labour pains, although it can be controlled and directed outwards to shake the hands instead. One man at Airport Vineyard Church, Toronto, proudly wears a T-shirt with the legend: 'I'm a JERK FOR JESUS!'

- **Uncontrollable laughter or wailing and inconsolable weeping**. The Blessing has been associated with extremes of laughter as well as the weeping that might be expected as part of intense Christian religious experience. The laughter ranges from polite giggles to roaring, hysterical, uncontrollable fits of mirth, such as a young child might display when tickled. This 'gut-busting' convulsive laughter disconnects the person from what is going on around them.

- **Apparent drunkenness**. Some people just feel a little giddy, others lose control of their limbs, as if drunk, and are unable to walk in a straight line or even stand, whilst otherwise being fully conscious. The Blessing has been described as drunkenness 'without the hangover and without the expense'. Sometimes people have had to be carried out to their cars after the church service has finished. This drunkenness has reputedly happened in public places, such as restaurants where people have slid off their chairs and rolled about on the floor – and been asked to leave – as well as within the church or home context. This is not the drunkenness of oblivion, but mind and body are temporarily disconnected.

- **Animal sounds**. Sometimes the Blessing involves a person making animal sounds. People have roared like lions, barked like dogs, brayed like donkeys, or even imitated Donald Duck! It has been suggested that the sounds have a physiological source in the 'Toronto Twitch'.

• **Intense physical activity**. People occasionally start running energetically around the church, jogging on the spot, bouncing up and down as if they are on a pogo-stick, even pretending to be 'red indians' or racing cars!

The external physical characteristics of the Blessing do not exhaust its meaning for the individual or church concerned, indeed these are surface phenomena generally reflecting what is reported to be a deeply meaningful, ecstatic religious experience. It may well be accompanied by 'prophetic' insights into the future, 'prophetic' announcements from God, 'prophetic' deep insight into their, or another's, problems, visions (sometimes of hell), and 'out of the body' mystical experiences. Sometimes the Blessing may be received without extraordinary outward signs. The worshipper may simply raise their hands and feel an immense sense of peace (Fearon 1994: 2).

The Background to the Blessing

Churches most likely to be affected by the Blessing are those of a Pentecostal or charismatic flavour. Pentecostalism as a mass movement began in the first decade of the twentieth century. It stressed the present availability of direct, powerful experience of the Holy Spirit, together with gifts and signs of the Spirit, such as speaking in tongues, miracles, healings and exorcism. By the mid 1920s classical Pentecostalism gave birth to the Assemblies of God and the Elim Church (presently numbering over 75,000 members). Pentecostalism took a new and surprising turn in the 1960s, when it began to affect all the major denominations, in the form of the Charismatic Renewal. Previously it had been Protestant, fundamentalist and sectarian, drawing mostly upon the working-class. Now (Neo-)Pentecostalism began to attract the middle-class intelligentsia and to take root more widely, even within the Roman Catholic Church. Unlike Classical Pentecostalism the Renewal Movement did not split off from mainstream churches, but remained within them as a spring-board for change. Charismatic Renewal expressed many of the increasingly inward-oriented, counter-cultural values of the late 1960s, including a thirst for authentic experience and supra-rational illumination, not tied to outdated dogmas and centred in the spontaneity of the present moment.

Since the peak of the Renewal Movement, probably in the late 1970s, an independent network of newly-formed Evangelical-Protestant charismatic churches known ori-ginally as 'house churches' or 'restorationist churches' has developed, partly as a response to the perceived growing theological liberalism of parts of the Charismatic Renewal Movement and the waning of its initial impetus. Now describing themselves as 'new churches', these churches or 'fellowships' often meet in hired halls for their exuberant, Spirit-centred, 'happy clappy' style of worship. Influential leaders within this 'new churches' network include Terry Virgo, Bryn Jones, John Noble and Gerald Coates. The 'new church' movement has also been influenced by such figures as the American ex-Quaker, charismatic leader John Wimber, with his stress on 'power encounter' with God's present-day 'signs and wonders'. John Wimber's nineteen 'Vineyard Fellowships' are now an important feature of the charismatic landscape in Britain. It has been estimated that the membership of the 'new churches' grew in the 1980s from about 250,000 to over 350,000, although they may have peaked in the early 1980s. In the meantime, Charismatic Renewal has entered a new phase within the mainstream churches; its worship has become less emotionally volatile and it has broadened its historical focus to include, for instance, Christian mysticism. Recently there have been attempts to forge stronger links between existing Evangelical churches and the 'new churches', spearheaded by Clive Calver of the Evangelical Alliance, and 'new churches' themselves have patched up many of their erstwhile differences (Roberts 1994: 34; Fearon 1994: 214–15).

The immediate pre-history of the Toronto Blessing revolves around the figure of 33–year-old, South African-born international Pentecostal evangelist, Rodney Howard-Browne, whose ministry has been widely associated with outbreaks of holy laughter. Howard-Browne was a seminal influence on the leadership of the Airport Vineyard, Toronto and on Randy Clark, the visiting speaker who acted as catalyst for the first outbreak of the Toronto Blessing at Airport Vineyard Church in January 1994. As early as April 1993 people had been travelling from the UK to witness Howard-Browne's extraordinary meetings (Roberts 1994: 17).

Most of the features of the Toronto Blessing have been reported within charismatic churches and meetings previously. They are not entirely new phenomena, although the intensity, frequency and spread of these features is said to be unparalleled in recent times. Also the phenomenon seems to have become more 'democratic', less dependent on the ministry of a specific leader of worship and more associated with a 'ministry team'.

The so-called 'Third Wave of the Spirit' in the mid 1980s, particularly associated with John Wimber's international 'power ministry', manifested itself in falling, uncontrollable laughter, shaking, weeping, and bouncing. Indeed the 'Wimber Wobbles' predated the 'Toronto Trots' by ten years, Wimber having first encountered such phenomena in 1979 (Lewis 1994: 3; MacNutt 1994: 2). Wimber's Vineyard

Churches have been no strangers to the phenomena of the Blessing in the last decade. Similar manifestations were reported at weekly prayer meetings at Digby Stuart College, south-west London, seven years ago: 'people were bouncing, convulsing, trembling, laughing, crying, and falling over' (*Tablet*, 20 August 1994, 1056). 'Slaying in the Spirit' was already prevalent in the Charismatic Renewal in the mid 1970s and was well known to Classical Pentecostalists. George Canty, an Elim leader, has drawn parallels with the 'glory fits' in early Pentecostal cottage meetings (*Direction*, October 1994, 41).

How Has it Spread?

Its proponents have spoken of the Blessing as a movement of the Spirit, spreading spontaneously from Toronto 'like a virus'. In fact its spread can be explained by more mundane factors reflecting an increasingly 'globalised' world. Modern electronic communications, in the form of national and international phone calls, faxes, and e-mail have played a significant part. Magazine articles, for instance in the evangelical magazine *Alpha*, newspaper and TV coverage, and popular paperbacks have helped its spread. Transatlantic air travel by large numbers of church leaders from Britain to see the phenomenon at first hand has also played an important role: Airport Vineyard is literally just at the end of the runway! By September 1994 over 4000 pastors, spouses and leaders had visited, and made their 'pilgrimage', from North America, Great Britain, Chile, Argentina, Switzerland, France, Germany, Scandinavia, South Africa, Nigeria, Kenya, Japan, New Zealand, Australia. British visitors to Airport Vineyard, Toronto have usually brought the Blessing with them on their return to Britain. Eleanor Mumford, wife of the South-West London Vineyard pastor, enthused HTB

with the Blessing on 29 May 1994, after her return from
Toronto. The tape of her talk has been itself widely circulated. Certain churches have become 'epicentres' of the
Blessing, to which curious leaders and members of other
churches have flocked for special week-night or late-Sunday-
evening meetings dominated by testimony about and experience of the Blessing, with up to 600 present (1200 at HTB).
The arrival of the Blessing generally depends on the presence
and initiative of sympathetic leaders within a church. Leaders
themselves, already charismatics or evangelicals, may often
first have come across the phenomenon through their own
churches' network – for instance, the Pioneer, New Fron-
tiers, or Covenant networks, which were substantially
involved – or at one of the epicentres. The Tuesday morning
'Leaders Prayer Meetings' during summer 1994 at one such
epicentre, Queen's Road Church, Wimbledon, were
attended by over 200 leaders per week, from all over Britain
and Europe. The Blessing was well on show at last summer's
large evangelical charismatic gatherings, such as New Wine
at Shepton Mallet, attracting 7000, and HTB's Week at
Morecambe Bay.

How is the Experience Shaped?[1]

Labelling the Experience

The experience labelled 'The Toronto Blessing' has been
interpreted by participating churches in broadly similar ways,
although the phenomena could be subject to quite different
interpretations: John and Charles Wesley, for instance, interpreted spontaneous uncontrollable laughter as the 'buffeting

---

[1] The structure of this section of the paper partly derives from Spickard's
(1993) categorisation of sociological approaches to religious experience.

of Satan' (John Wesley's Journal: 9 and 21 May 1740) and as a terrorising experience. It appears that in some cases, at least, the raw experience precedes any knowledge of the Blessing and that in these instances it is not a learned behaviour, but instead attributable to psychological causes. This, of course, is not to preclude the possibility that the Holy Spirit may also be operating. An incident connected with the ministry of US faith healer, Kathryn Kuhlmann, earlier this century is sometimes cited as an example of what can happen: as Kuhlmann travelled up in a lift to the conference hall at which she was due to speak, the chefs on an intermediate floor spontaneously fell to the ground. This is recounted in *The Anointing*, by Benny Hinn, one of the seminal figures behind the Toronto Blessing. It was cited by the pastor at the late-Sunday-evening meeting at Queen's Road Church on 13 November 1994. The Toronto Blessing has similarly, it is claimed, arrived spontaneously at a number of churches (Roberts 1994: 32, 39, 146).

Some phenomena associated with the Blessing have been interpreted differently by non-participating churches, or even historically within Charismatic Renewal. Roaring like a lion has been interpreted by some as a prophetic symbol referring to Jesus as the 'Lion of Judah', in one case breaking the power of the Dragon over the Chinese people (Eleanor Mumford, HTB, 29 May 1994), in another case 'literally chasing out the power of sin and declaring His righteous anger at the remaining captivity of (the recipient's) soul' (Chevreau 1994: 187–8). Others, referring instead to C. S. Lewis' *The Lion, The Witch, and The Wardrobe*, have interpreted the roaring as a sign that 'Aslan is coming' (*HTB in Focus*, 14 August 1994: 7). Still others have seen it as a sign that God is 'putting some backbone back into our men' (ibid: 4)! Clifford Hill has criticised the phenomenon, noting that the prophet Jeremiah associates roaring like a lion with 'the occult spirit of Babylon' (*Dunamis* Autumn 1994, no. 89: 11). The phenomenon of 'falling' has been labelled in different ways. The traditional description of falling within Pentecostalism is 'being slain in the Spirit'. Where falling occurs as part of the Blessing its proponents prefer terms such as 'resting in the Spirit', because the older term does not do justice to the sense of peace and the divine enlivening and empowerment that is said to be received (MacNutt 1994: 24, 27; Chevreau 1994: 15).

Some phenomena have not found widespread acceptance within participating churches. John Wimber, for instance, has been concerned about the occurrence of barnyard animal and other zoological noises, and is reported as saying: 'I [do not] see it as something that ought to be endorsed, embraced, affirmed or accepted by the Church. I think we ought to ignore it' (*Church Times*, 30 September 1994: 8). The Elim Churches magazine *Direction* similarly had hesitations about animal noises on the grounds that God only 'humbles but never humiliates those who truly seek Him' (October 1994: 6). Even those who initially welcomed animal noises as part of the Blessing may, with hindsight, discount these phenomena. Gerald Coates has questioned whether convulsions are a valid part of the Blessing, on the grounds that most, if not all, Scripture references to convulsions attribute them to a demonic source (*Renewal*, November 1994: 25).

Getting the Idea

Normally a person will experience the Blessing only after accepting that the experience exists and what it means, or, at least, after weighing up carefully the idea of the experience. This experimental 'Beroean' (Acts 17:10f) attitude to the idea of the Blessing is actively reinforced by the leadership who urge those interested to sit and 'look on and weigh up things'. One twenty-three-year-old freelance journalist told how she had said to God: 'Lord, I don't understand what's happening. If it's from you help me to understand it'. Where significant others – co-religionists, respected 'level-headed' church leaders, friends or family – have already accepted the Blessing as a desirable and beneficial phenomenon a positive outcome to the weighing-up process may be predicted; in particular 'the leaders are the gatekeepers and what they will allow, the people feel confident to allow' (Vineyard Toronto leaflet 20 April 1994). As Mary Jo Neitz concluded in her work on Roman Catholic Charismatics: 'what one finds is an interplay between "what is believed to be possible" and "what is", through which a general belief becomes meaningful for an individual in a particular situation' (Neitz 1987: 99).

Perhaps the most important ways by which people are introduced to the idea of the Blessing are by means of introductory talks by the leadership and personal testimonies by recipients of the experience, within services and meetings. Some of these testimonies have been reproduced in popular paperback treatments of the Blessing (for instance, Chevreau 1994: 145–204). Sometimes roving microphones are taken to people already 'on the carpet' and an informal interview is broadcast over the PA system; this practice amplifies the phenomenon in more ways than one! Interpretations of the Blessing vary, but include references to a sense of the awesome Presence of God contrasted with human sinfulness, his sovereign authority, his[2] joy, his peace, his nearness, his pleasure, his power, his brilliant glory. The Blessing is said to be accompanied by such features as a deeper love for and intimacy with God, a new love for Jesus, a greater sense

---

[2] Sometimes reference is made to Jesus, sometimes to God: the term 'Lord' is ambiguous. Sexually-inclusive language is not used of the godhead.

of expectancy, forgiveness, emotional healing, the healing of relationships, physical healings, a new passion to read Scripture which itself 'comes to life', a desire and courage to witness, an increased desire to pray, commitment to evangelism, boldness to challenge unrighteousness, injustice and corruption in society, and, occasionally, deliverance from demonic influence. Sometimes the physical phenomena are interpreted as prophetic symbolic action on the part of God who is, for instance, believed to be (literally) 'shaking' the recipient out of their complacency and self-sufficiency or demonstrating 'human weakness' to induce humility (*HTB in Focus*, 14 August 1994: 9; MacNutt 1994: 30, 173). It is generally described as being primarily for the already converted and a 'time of refreshment'. Sometimes people are warned that it might be, rarely, a bad experience, if they have not previously repented.

There is inevitably a high degree of informal social pressure on people to follow the lead of co-religionists who have already experienced the Blessing, reflected sociologically in frequent references by the leadership to the presence of the 'power of God' in the worship setting. This is accentuated at some churches by the practice of removing chairs during 'ministry time' whilst many are standing to receive the Blessing or have already fallen; those still seated easily begin to feel 'the odd one out'.

Learning to have the Blessing

Although favourable ideas about the Blessing are usually an important pre-condition for receiving and sharing the experience, any religious experience is also shaped by less conceptual means. Techniques and practical tips are passed on as part of a process of practical personal guidance for the individual who is trying to receive the experience, much as a driving instructor helps the learner translate theory into practice on the road. Some of the practical advice comes from reading religious magazine articles (Poloma and Pendleton 1989: 428) and popular paperbacks about the Blessing. Many of the services and meetings within which it occurs are orchestrated in such a way that early on there are practical demonstrations of individuals being prayed for and falling, often after they have publicly testified about the experience (Roberts 1994: 78). Practical guidance is later more personally mediated when members of the (lay) 'ministry team' pray in pairs with those wishing to receive the blessing. They may or may not make physical contact with the individual, but one of them will usually place or agitate his or her hand near the person's forehead, whilst another will be ready to act as 'catcher'. The ministry team will normally have been through an 'apprenticeship' period (Roberts 1994: 69) and have been trained according to certain accepted guidelines within that specific church, often borrowed from other churches. Vineyard Church Toronto's 'Suggested Ministry Tips' (20 April 1994), augmented by HTB's 'Ministry Values' (15 June 1994), have been widely circulated. These include the following 'Tips for Praying for People':

- If the person is one of the 'hard ones' you might help them (by calming) their fears over loss of control by helping them know what to expect. For example, let them know that they will have a clear mind, that they can usually stop the process at any point if they want to, and that the Spirit comes in waves.

- Some people have 'fear of falling' issues. Help them to sit down or to fall carefully, especially if they have back problems, pregnancy or fear of falling.

Members of ministry teams will encourage those they are praying with to face their fears – 'the fear of deception; the fear of being hurt again or not receiving at all; the fear of losing control'. They will urge them to 'focus on the Lord, not on falling' and to 'give the Holy Spirit permission to do with you what He wants to do' (Vineyard Toronto 20 April 1994). Often those ministering will repeat short phrases such as: 'Receive His power', 'The Lord is with you', 'More of your Spirit, God' or 'Breathe in the Spirit', which are designed to increase receptivity. Perhaps the most important part of the technique is the advice to stop analysing and 'just relax and ask him to come' (Lawrence 1992: 131; Roberts 1994: 141).

Tired Leaders, Tired Churches – Why Have Churches Invested in the Toronto Blessing?

Investment in the Blessing has been costly in terms of time, energy and, not least, money: transatlantic air trips to Toronto do not exactly come cheaply. £3500 was raised by Sunderland Christian Centre for this purpose in a single offering (Roberts 1994: 54). This level of investment suggests that the Blessing is expected to have tangible benefits for the individuals and particularly churches involved. These are not confined to spiritual benefits. Indeed the Blessing may have come at a strategically useful time in the life-cycle of the churches concerned and the careers of their leaders. In addition, it may be what the 'charismatic market' demands. The advent of the Blessing at this time makes sense when it is viewed alongside two major problems affecting charismatic churches: the precariousness of their market and the precariousness of charisma (Wallis 1984: 86–118).

A Precarious Market

One plausible reason for churches investing in the Blessing is as a means of safeguarding their share of a relatively static market. Evangelical charismatics have for some years begun to perceive each other less as competitors and more as sales-men/women of a similar product, simply 'marginally differ-entiated' between almost identical brands. They have also tried to forge links with non-charismatic Evangelicals. This has probably partly been a response to the precariousness of their market. In spite of intensive investment in evangelism and church-planting the charismatic customer-base has not grown as much as anticipated in recent years. One ex-planation for this might be that the market has been fully-exploited: the market for charismatic Christianity may be more limited than they imagine. The JIM (Jesus in Me) Mission in July 1994 spearheaded by Elim and the Assemblies of God aimed to mobilise 250,000 Christians to reach 250,000 souls for Christ. In the event only between 20,000 and 30,000 responded with some sort of faith-response (*Alpha* July 1994: 12, 13). At the same time, charismatic churches are suffering the perennial problem that faces every new movement: boredom and apathy on the part of the second generation. Churches risk losing their teenagers who have grown up accustomed to charismatic phenomena.

Many charismatic churches seem to have seized on the Blessing as a means of retaining their customers. They have had to become more 'sensitive to their market'. Significantly, the Blessing is perceived as predominantly a 'time of refresh-ing' for the already-converted. One response to market stag-nation is to give the customer 'more of the same' or more of what attracted them in the first place, rekindling the original fire. The Blessing has been described as 'the spiritual equivelant [sic] of a seven-course dinner at a fancy restaurant'

(*Alpha* September 1994: 4). Charismatic customers demand something more than they could get in virtually any other church. The initial attractions of the charismatic renewal included the sense of novelty and excitement that it gave, the direct, unmediated and unpredictable encounter with God that it offered, and the heady experience of the power of a God who was anything but dead. In many respects this represented a reaction against key characteristics of modern society. Ironically, as we shall see below, charismatic churches have been themselves increasingly infiltrated by the modernity which is so inimical to charisma. The Blessing has come at a time when, as leading Baptist minister Rob Warner put it, 'the fresh sparkle of novelty (had) been increasingly replaced by familiarity': the Spirit had been domesticated and tamed (*Renewal* November 1994: 10). Sandy Millar, vicar of HTB, spoke for many when he said: '(renewal) was looking very tired . . . these manifestations are restoring to us the intimacy with God for which we cried out when we first became Christians' (*Church Times* 23 September 1994: 7). Many have spoken of 'returning to their first love' or of 'falling in love with Jesus all over again' (Chevreau 1994: 18, 182).

Another response to market stagnation is to adjust to shifts in consumer preferences. Where people are under increasing stress and risk 'burnout' in their working lives, it is not surprising that the religious consumer may prefer not to be constantly under pressure from their church to be hyperactive for the Lord, but, instead, to be attracted by a phenomenon that gives them the opportunity to 'rest in the Spirit'. Eleanor Mumford spoke of 'many very weary pastors' and their 'even more weary wives' flocking to Toronto (HTB 29 May 1994; see also Chevreau 1994: 19; Roberts 1994: 163).

Precarious Charisma

One reason why the leadership of charismatic churches has been so interested in promoting the Blessing may be their hope that it will renew the charismatic appeal of their leadership and reverse tendencies to become just like any other organisation. In the world of sociology the term 'charismatic' has a slightly different meaning to the one we have presupposed so far. When the term is used of a leader it usually denotes an extraordinary individual considered to have exceptional, even superhuman, powers or qualities. The successful charismatic leader generates a personal following, based on his or her perceived ability to resolve certain problems or crises for the followers. Charisma dynamically transcends both the ordinary routine of everyday life and traditional religious apparatus. However, charisma is intrinsically volatile and ephemeral. It typically evaporates or becomes 'routinised' over the course of time, especially when the leaders age and die, as is starting to happen within charismatic renewal. Rob Warner has noted that 'First-generation renewal has been around for more than a generation. Several early leaders have died, others are drawing near to retirement, and so need to begin to hand over the reins' (*Renewal* November 1994: 10). One of the special features of 'charismatic churches' is the way in which the property of charisma, in the sociological sense, is perceived to be shared by the membership and to permeate the whole group.

If you had been asked to classify the leaders of charismatic 'new churches' in terms of the type of authority they exercised, then, in the early days, you might have placed them towards the 'charismatic authority' end of the spectrum. Although one has to reckon with some retrospective mythologising, it appears that their followers were frequently on first-name terms with them and organisation was relatively free and unstructured (Walker 1989: 53, 58, 61, 283). Nowadays many of the leaders, at national and local levels, have begun to wake up to the fact that their leadership style has drifted along the spectrum and become less charismatic and more bureaucratic, akin to that exercised by captains of industry. Baptist minister and author of a popular paperback on the Blessing, Guy Chevreau, confessed that in recent years he had immersed himself in books about 'leadership, innovation, infrastructure, time management, goal setting and strategic planning' (Chevreau 1994: 12; cf. 184). Chevreau suggests that countless church leaders have, with the best of intentions, 'run aground, if not exhausted themselves and the churches they serve' thanks to the influence of 'growth and business management strategies' (Chevreau 1994: 206).

Inevitably, for charisma to survive, albeit in attenuated form, it must be institutionalised in more 'efficient' and 'rational' ways such as this. Nevertheless this still leaves a series of problems for charismatic churches. If the charismatic movement has been partly a reaction against modernity, the increasing adoption of distinctly modern management styles by the leadership is bound to stimulate nostalgia for a more charismatic leadership style. Leaders, often close to burnout because of the new leadership styles, have an extra incentive to turn back the clock. For some, the Toronto Blessing has given the opportunity for having a kind of religious 'mid-life crisis' in which they have radically re-evaluated the direction of their ministries. Ken Costa, HTB churchwarden, confessed that 'we've tried might and power and organisation of the church — and we've seen nothing but the decline of every form of our expression of love towards God' (*HTB in Focus*, 14 August 1994: 9). Fort Wayne Vineyard pastor Ron Allen's description of his departure for Toronto is highly symbolic: 'I left my computer (and) took my bible' (Chevreau 1994: 150). With the help of the transfusion of the Blessing leaders have begun to renew their charismatic appeal. Hot-foot from Toronto, they offer a dynamic new phenomenon that they hope will turn their churches, and indeed the world, 'upside down' in the spirit of Acts 17:6.

Paradoxically, the Toronto Blessing is itself very much part and parcel of the modern world. Its rapid spread owes a lot to the latest communications technology and the availability of mass transatlantic air travel. At a more profound level, its proponents speak of it in pragmatic terms that reflect the functional rationality that dominates Western societies. 'If it works, trust it!' seems to be the message. 'It is not means, but the end that is of consequence' (Chevreau 1994: 143–4). As with other forms of fundamentalism, the Blessing is both antimodern and distinctively modern.

Why Has the Blessing Taken this Form?

The Blessing could have taken other forms. For instance, religious consumer interest could have been revived by means of snake-handling or walking on red-hot coals, phenomena already extant within fringe evangelical groups in the US. Instead, the Blessing is characterised by such features as bodily disinhibition, a strong sense of God being 'in control', and, at times, a mystical sense that the experience of God cannot be expressed in human language. I want to suggest that each of these three features could have been predicted in the light of socio-economic and cultural changes affecting the churches concerned.

From Fasting to Pogoing – Changing Attitudes to Bodily Disinhibition

Until recently, evangelical attitudes to the body have been very strait-laced and restrained. Evangelicals have been expected always to be in control of their bodies and their emotions which are 'for the Lord' (Synnott 1992: 91). If Evangelicals of previous generations were to witness the (spiritual) drunkenness sometimes associated with the Blessing they might well turn in their graves. HTB has had to reassure taxi drivers that their fares are ' "not drunk as you suppose" and safe to have in the taxi' (Roberts 1994: 33–4). Although the mind is clear, the body is overtaken by spiritual drunkenness, and behaves as if inebriated by alcohol (Fearon 1994: 27). Old-style Evangelicals might also be unhappy that the practice of totally abstaining from alcohol has gone out of fashion in many Evangelical churches (Hunter 1987: 58–9), especially those that are charismatic (Walker 1983: 96; Walker 1989: 97). Alcohol-induced drunkenness is not approved of, but drinking that leads to lesser degrees of bodily disinhibition is no longer necessarily castigated. The body has begun to be experienced as something that can be enjoyed, rather than, as before, feared and watched at all times lest it get out of control. Evangelical charismatics have increasingly adopted a positive and holistic view of the human person, in contrast to earlier, dualistic and Cartesian, views that devalued the body and treated it like a (dangerous) machine. This is reflected in the holistic orientation of charismatic healing ministry (Neitz 1987: 237–8) and in modern Evangelical attitudes to sex which no longer believe that 'Sex is dirty ... Sex is disgusting ... Sex is degrading ... Save it for your wife!' (Chalke in *Alpha* December 1994: 39).

During the second half of the twentieth century, in particular, attitudes to bodily disinhibition have undergone a sea-change throughout society. Historically, capitalism had demanded self-discipline, restraint, the subordination of animal passions, frugality and regularity (including the bowels!) from its workforce and this had been reflected in the inner-worldly asceticism of the 'Protestant Ethic', which remained influential long after its Puritan roots were forgotten (Turner 1984: 64–5, 218; 1992: 196–7). The Protestant Ethic was eventually undermined by the 'new capitalism' dating from the early decades of the twentieth century, which needed 'to stimulate a demand for pleasure and play' amongst consumers (Bell 1976: 75; Turner 1984: 25, 172). Consumers, with the help of easy credit, came to expect instant, rather than deferred, gratification. The 1960s counter culture replaced 'goodness morality' with the 'fun morality' of a more 'permissive society' (Bell 1976: 71). The result is that the late capitalist consumer is expected to be permanently unsatiated and 'seething with desire for new things and experiences' (Simpson 1993: 156).

The relatively new evangelical attitudes to relaxation of bodily restraints reflect these wider–socio–economic changes, which, given the strength of traditional evangelical attitudes, have taken some time to percolate through, although they had already been previewed in the demonstrative 'happy clappy' worship of charismatic churches. 'All my life I've longed to be naughty', Eleanor Mumford confessed to HTB. It was the Blessing that finally permitted her to 'roll about on the floor like a drunk woman'! Frugality and fasting seem to have gone out of fashion, instead it is as if the worshipper is invited to a high-spirited party. God is (no longer) 'a god of moderation in all things'.

Not surprisingly, the Toronto Blessing reflects and reinforces some of the features of consumerist society. Pastors teach that recipients should not be satisfied with just one experience of the Blessing: 'don't be afraid to come for more and more and more'. Like the material abundance of consumer society the Blessing is not in short supply! The consumer goals of happiness, health and personal fulfilment painlessly accompany the Blessing. Indeed, secular therapists have been impressed by the way in which the Blessing shortcuts many of their methods. The theological background to the Blessing downplays more mainstream traditional Christian teaching that speaks in terms of self-giving, self-sacrifice and self-denial. John Wimber has been criticised for neglecting the cross and suffering in his own teaching and both Rodney Howard-Browne and Benny Hinn, long-time friend of Airport Vineyard pastor John Arnott, have been associated with the 'health and wealth' 'prosperity gospel' of the 'Word of Faith' movement (Roberts 1994: 62, 96–9; Fearon 1994: 105–7). In such ways the bodily disinhibition associated with the Blessing appears to fit and reflect the consumerist society of modern Britain. One of the acknowledged dangers for the Blessing is that within this context of 'commodity culture' it will be treated merely as 'a trip for its own sake' and eventually discarded for the next 'latest thing' (Fearon 1994: 190).

Simultaneously, the bodily disinhibition of the Blessing might also be interpreted as a form of resistance to increasing societal, or even, in some cases, church, control over the body. The human body can sometimes become a 'source of playful energies' and a 'site of resistance' to societal over-regulation of the body (McGuire 1990; Turner 1992). This may help to explain one of the functions of the Blessing. In spite of signs of economic recovery, British consumers in 1994 still felt constrained to spend modestly and carefully. The *Guardian* reported in November 1994 that 'Barclaycard says shoppers intend to emulate Scrooge'. After the credit-financed 'spend . . . spend' 1980s, consumers, often now with 'negative equity' mortgages, preferred to hold on to their savings. This was still perceived to be a time of economic self-restraint. Some workers, who found themselves having to begin to work on Sundays, experienced the invasion of their erstwhile leisure time (Richter 1994). The experience of the Blessing represents one way in which consumers and workers were able, temporarily at least, to escape, through a playful form of religion, some of these economic constraints.

The Blessing, in some cases, represents a response to over-heavy regulation of the body by churches. The 'shepherding' or 'covering' practised by some new churches has sometimes extended to control by the leadership of a person's love life or place of residence (Walker 1987: 201–2; Walker 1989: 285–93, 177–88; Enroth 1992). MacNutt describes how a woman found release, through being overcome by the Spirit, after experiencing the strictest form of shepherding for a period of eight years (MacNutt 1994: 69).

God is not a Gentleman! – Changing Attitudes to Divine Gender Roles?

The God of the Toronto Blessing is strongly characterised as a macho male. This is a God who is dynamic and forceful and very much in control. Proponents of the Blessing have repeatedly stated that the old idea that 'God is a gentleman' (both polite and English!) is out of date and inaccurate. It is repeatedly claimed that there is no biblical basis for the belief that 'the Holy Spirit is a gentleman, and does nothing without our consent' (Chevreau 1994: 101) nor anything 'to embarrass you' (Roberts 1994: 159). 'God is not a wimpish fop, but a red-blooded male' seems to be the message. Equally, the church leadership needs to have some male 'back-bone' put back into it by the Blessing (Mary Pytches, *HTB in Focus*, 14 August 1994).

The Toronto Blessing appears to be, consciously or unconsciously, part of a move to re-masculinise the church. The reader who is used to thinking of the institutional churches as bastions of patriarchy and resistance to women's ministry may be surprised to find the argument framed in these terms. Nevertheless, feminisation has affected most churches, particularly since the nineteenth century. As the process of secularisation has increasingly deprived religion of social power and restricted its influence to the private sphere of home and family so God and Jesus have been depicted in gentler terms (Roberts 1984: 356–7). The activity of God has been seen less in terms of control and domination and more as characterised by caring and nurturing. 'Gentle Jesus, meek and mild' has been the order of the day (Fearon 1994: 139).

Receiving the Blessing involves a willingness to surrender control to a God 'who is in control and sovereign'. 'God is not a gentleman, God is God' (*Alpha* September 1994: 3). The secret is to 'give God the reins and let him reign'. One recipient reported that 'the Lord came . . . and overpowered me in such a way that I know His ability to give is greater than my unwitting ability to resist' (Chevreau 1994: 158). Rodney Howard-Browne warned his 'Signs and Wonders' audience at the Wembley Conference Centre: 'some of you are going to get hit tonight [just] because you're sitting in the wrong seat!' (13 December 1994). Being 'overcome by the Spirit' is interpreted as 'an extraordinary demonstration of God's omnipotence' (MacNutt 1994: 46). Here we have a God made in *man's* image, the 'deification of unilateral power', reflecting masculinist notions of the nature of power (Clack 1994).

Whilst the Blessing helps to re-masculinise God and the (male) church leadership, obversely it places the ordinary recipient of the Blessing into a fairly passive, traditionally feminine role, which, particularly as far as women are concerned, is likely to be disempowering. The relationship between Jesus and the worshipper is analogous to that between husband and wife. The Church is identified as the Bride of Christ, for whom Jesus is coming. Quasi-sexual imagery is sometimes used to describe the Blessing experience. One (female) recipient reported: 'I'm actually just enjoying Jesus, and have the sense He's enjoying me' (Chevreau 1994: 161). Note the asymmetry of the relationship symbolised in the upper case used for the divine personal pronoun. In some cases recipients describe their experience in terms of the labour of child-birth (Chevreau 1994: 159). Ironically, the more passive the worshipper is, the more impersonal is the Divine-human relationship, such that the Holy Spirit eventually becomes more an 'it' than a 'He', as we shall see below. The experience does not demand complete passivity from the recipient, since this would make it an impersonal affair, instead of a genuine relationship with the Holy Spirit.

Charismatic Mysticism – Changing Communication Patterns

The Toronto Blessing is essentially a non-verbal form of religious experience. It is true that it can be accompanied by words of various kinds of prophecy and recipients are encouraged to verbalise and write down what they have experienced, but at its heart the Blessing is non-verbal in form. In fact it is sometimes described in mystical terms (Fearon 1994: 199). It has sometimes been compared to the experience of Christian mystics such as Teresa of Avila (MacNutt 1994: 18, 35, 88). Interestingly, Jonathan Edwards, eighteenth-century evangelist and one of the historical heroes of the Toronto Blessing movement, has himself been described as an 'evangelical mystic' (Chevreau 1994: 71). Sarah Edwards, his wife, reports that 'the glory of God seemed to be all, and in all, and to swallow up every wish and desire of my heart' and that her 'soul has been as it were overwhelmed, and swallowed up with light and love, a sweet solace altogether unspeakable . . .' (cited in Chevreau 1994: 79, 80, 85).

Mysticism is a mode of religious experience typically involving such features as a sense of oneness with all things, a sense of timelessness and spacelessness, a sense of deep and profound peace, the dissolution of sense of self, and a sense of ineffability – the mystical experience is beyond human language and in some cases the mind may simply be conscious of 'the void' (Spilka 1985: 176–8; Hay 1987: 91–2). Rudolf Otto characterised mysticism as in essence 'the overstressing of the non-rational or supra-rational elements in religion' (Otto 1923: 22). Evangelicals are, however, keen to distance themselves from what they term 'Eastern mysticism' and its 'disengagement of the mind' (*Alpha* October 1994: 6). Ironically, the 'Word of Faith' movement, with which some of the Blessing's progenitors have been associated, has been criticised for the 'strong strands of Eastern mysticism' within its teachings (Fearon 1994: 108).

Charismatics claim that they have been taught by the Blessing that they had become 'too matey with God'. They have rediscovered that God will not fit human 'boxes' and bursts out of human thought categories: God is 'supra-rational'. They distance themselves from the 'rational evangelical god of the intellect' (Poloma 1989: 418; Roberts 1994: 183). Recipients of the Blessing sometimes describe their experience, in impersonal terms, as 'being surrounded by the light of God', as being 'transparent with light', as 'resting under the cloak of his glory', as a 'state of blissful abandonment' or like 'electric current'. The Sea of Faith returns in waves of power! Sometimes recipients report 'out-of-body' experiences: Belma Vardy reported seeing herself 'walking in a lush green pasture, hand in hand with Jesus' (Chevreau 1994: 179–80). One man reported that, whilst overcome by the Spirit, 'he experienced a sensation as if he were melting into the chairs' (White 1989: 15–16).

Guy Chevreau of Airport Vineyard Toronto suggests that the phenomena of the Blessing are, as it were, 'an unfamiliar, non-verbal language (which) is being used to describe and declare what the Spirit of God is doing in people's lives' (1994: 28). Indeed the *cognoscenti* can recognise 'an extensive repertoire of kinetic language that seems to symbolize the Spirit's desires and actions' (Chevreau 1994: 193). Chevreau recognises that some religious experiences are beyond the power of words to describe. Interestingly, he cites Aquinas, who while saying Mass in December 1273 was so moved that he never wrote or dictated another word in his life (Chevreau 1994: 42)! Normally verbose and articulate pastors have similarly been virtually reduced to temporary silence by their experience of the Blessing. Some recipients of the Blessing 'struggle for words that adequately describe what they have experienced', others resort to poetic language (Chevreau 1994: 212).

Although charismatic Evangelicals are careful not to downplay the centrality of the Bible, the written word of God in their religion, and search for biblical precedents for the Blessing, they recognise that, as Gerald Coates put it, 'when God comes in power, non-biblical things (can) take place!' (*Alpha* July 1994: 46). It is claimed that 'a touch of God himself must surely be more important than the "Word of God" being read' (Pytches in MacNutt 1994: 7). 'Rigid biblical literalism is not conducive to the Spirit of revival' (Chevreau 1994: 53). God does not limit himself to working in ways that can be unambiguously 'prooftexted' from the Scriptures. In this sense charismatic Evangelicals are not consistent biblical fundamentalists. In fact biblical fundamentalism has proved difficult to sustain amongst Evangelicals generally. Rob Warner has complained that 'a growing number of evangelical Christians today are biblically illiterate' (*Renewal* November 1994: 11). The eclectic and trite nature of some of the words of prophecy given by people experiencing the Blessing reinforces this conclusion. The influence of the 'power evangelicalism' associated with John Wimber has further helped to marginalise and de-emphasise Scripture (McGrath 1993: 160).

It is not without significance that Evangelicals have, in the Blessing, enthusiastically embraced a non-verbal form of religious experience and expression. They live in a postmodern world, in which there are no privileged vantage points and relativism denies the validity of transcultural 'truth'. Religious beliefs have been reduced to the status of mere opinions and 'one person's opinion is as good as another's'. Although Evangelicals sincerely believe that they have 'absolute truth' on their side, postmodern society cannot admit this possibility. One response, already predicted by the sociologist Ernest Gellner, is that religious expression may dissolve in this way into 'speaking in tongues or (logically) silence' (Gellner 1992: 36). Paradoxically, charismatic Evangelical churches may be reflecting two quite different responses to postmodernity: fundamentalism (Walker 1989: 130) and either meta-language or non-language.

It is also plausible that this essentially non-verbal Blessing reflects the increasing difficulty Evangelicals have in making their gospel intelligible to modern society. As Steve Chalke remarked: (as Evangelicals) 'too often we've preached "The Word", but when we've not been understood, our response has simply been to shout louder' (*Alpha* October 1994: 35). Another response, I would suggest, has been to stop shouting and settle for the Toronto Blessing's essentially non-verbal approach.

Intellectual middle-class Evangelicals may, however, face a further tension, which the Blessing may help to mediate. It is not simply that *other* people find the Gospel unintelligible, Evangelicals themselves may be finding traditional religious language implausible when they themselves are full participants in modern culture – because, for instance, of their everyday work situations (Hervieu–Léger 1993: 146). The world of 'information superhighways' seems a million miles from the world of faith. If intellectual middle–class Evangelicals are finding that the Gospel does not seem to be 'speaking the same language' any more, one solution is to adopt the inarticulate meta–language of glossolalia, another is to embrace the non–verbal Toronto Blessing. Both solutions avoid head–on engagement with the language of modernity. In this way the Blessing can be seen as helping to mediate the acute contradiction between their religious 'cultural capital' and the day–to–day realities of living and working in the 1990s.

Not every church in Britain, as we have seen, has warmed to the Toronto Blessing. But, for those that have, it has been a timely arrival. For sociological reasons, if no other, the Toronto Blessing, from Airport Vineyard, touched down at just the right time!

Bibliography

Bell, Daniel (1976) *The Cultural Contradictions of Capitalism*, London: Heinemann.

Chevreau, Guy (1994) *Catch the Fire: the Toronto Blessing, an experience of renewal and revival*, London: Marshall Pickering.

Clack, Beverley (1994) 'Omnipotence, masculinity and God', paper given at the Philosophy of Religion seminar, King's College London, 8 December.

Enroth, Ronald (1992) *Churches that Abuse*, Grand Rapids: Zondervan.

Fearon, Mike (1994) *A Breath of Fresh Air*, Guildford: Eagle.

Gellner, Ernest (1992) *Postmodernism, Reason and Religion*, London: Routledge.

Hay, David (1987) *Exploring Inner Space: is God still possible in the twentieth century?* London: Mowbray.

Hervieu-Léger, Danièle (1993) 'Present-day emotional renewals: the end of secularization or the end of religion? in Swatos 1993: 129–48.

Hunter, J. D. (1987) *Evangelicalism: the coming generation*, Chicago: University of Chicago Press.

Lawrence, Peter H. (1992) *Doing What Comes Supernaturally*, Eastbourne: Kingsway.

Lewis, David (1994) *Christian Herald*, 15 October.

MacNutt, Francis (1990, new prologue, 1994) *Overcome by the Spirit*, Guildford: Eagle.

McGrath, Alister (1993) *Evangelicalism and the Future of Christianity*, London: Hodder and Stoughton.

McGuire, Meredith B. (1990) 'Religion and the body: rematerializing the human body in the social sciences of religion', *Journal for the Scientific Study of Religion 29*, no. 3, 283–96.

Neitz, Mary J. (1987) *Charisma and Community: a study of religious commitment within the charismatic renewal*, Oxford: Transaction Books.

Otto, Rudolf (1923) *The Idea of the Holy*, London: Oxford University Press.

Poloma, Margaret M. and Pendleton, Brian F. (1989) 'Religious experiences, evangelism, and institutional growth within the Assemblies of God', *Journal for the Scientific Study of Religion 28*, no. 4, 415–31.

Richter, Philip J. (1994) 'Seven days' trading make one weak? The Sunday trading issue as an index of secularization', *British Journal of Sociology 45*, no. 3, 333–48.

Roberts, David (1994) *The 'Toronto Blessing'*, Eastbourne: Kingsway.

Roberts, K. A. (1984) *Religion in Sociological Perspective*, Chicago: Dorsey Press.

Simpson, John H. (1993) 'Religion and the body: sociological themes and prospects', in Swatos 1993: 149–64.

Spickard, James V. (1993) 'For a sociology of religious experience', in Swatos 1993: 109–28.

Spilka, B., Hood, R. W. Jr. and Gorsuch, R. L. (1985) *The Psychology of Religion: an empirical approach*, Englewood Cliffs, NJ: Prentice-Hall.

Synnott, Anthony (1992) 'Tomb, temple, machine and self: the social construction of the body', *British Journal of Sociology 43*, no. 1, 79–110.

Swatos, William H. Jr. (1993) *A Future for Religion? new paradigms for social analysis*, London: Sage.

Turner, Bryan S. (1984) *The Body and Society: explorations in social theory*, Oxford: Basil Blackwell.

Turner, Bryan S. (1992) *Regulating Bodies: essays in medical sociology*, London: Routledge.

Walker, Andrew (1983) 'Pentecostal power: the "Charismatic Renewal Movement" and the politics of pentecostal experience', in Eileen Barker, *Of Gods and Men*, Macon, GA: Mercer University Press, 89–108.

Walker, Andrew (1987) 'Fundamentalism and modernity: the Restoration Movement in Britain', in Caplan, L. (ed.) *Studies in Religious Fundamentalism*, Albany, NY: State University of New York Press.

Walker, Andrew (1989) *Restoring the Kingdom: the radical Christianity of the House Church Movement*, London: Hodder and Stoughton.

Wallis, Roy (1984) *The Elementary Forms of the New Religious Life*, London: Routledge & Kegan Paul.

White, John (1989) *When the Spirit Comes with Power*, London: Hodder and Stoughton.

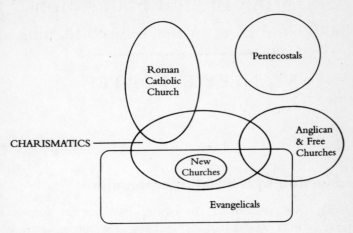

The Charismatics (size of circles does not indicate numbers)

2
Shaking the Biblical Foundations?
The Biblical Basis for the Toronto Blessing

STANLEY E. PORTER

Introduction to Biblical Interpretation

That there is a concern for the biblical basis for the Toronto Blessing cannot be denied. As Peel says, 'Scripture alone is our final authority. It commands us to weigh all things and test the spirits whether they be of God or not' (1994: 1). Discussion of the Bible, of supposedly similar biblical phenomena, and of arguably parallel contemporary manifestations are consequently topics of interest in various articles and books, at seminars, and in services associated with the Toronto Blessing. Several of the leading churches experiencing the blessing have referred to themselves as 'word and spirit' churches, with the word to be as important as Spirit (see for instance Roberts August 1994: 17, citing Bryn Jones; Roberts October 1994: 3, citing Dave Holden; Lancaster October 1994: 7). The impression at least is that those who have the Toronto Blessing are seeking in some way to explain the biblical basis for their experience. But discussion of the Bible is not the same as providing a solid biblical foundation, and the ability to quote biblical passages or supposed proof-texts is not the same as establishing a biblical position, and

reading the Bible is not the same as understanding and apply-
ing it correctly. Being able to interpret the Bible in a responsible way so as to provide a biblical foundation for a given
belief or practice is serious business, and requires a well-
considered approach to the Bible. Any Christian group wishing to establish its belief and practice as biblically-based,
however, must pay attention to such issues.

That interpretation of the Bible is not as easy as simply
quoting a few well-selected verses or prooftexts can be seen
in the following examples. The first is used in a humourous
way to make a serious point. Matthew 27:3 says that Judas
'went away and hanged himself'.[1] In Luke 10:37, Jesus says
'Go and do likewise'. Do these verses constitute a biblical
injunction to suicide? They are nothing of the sort, but
their quotation together does illustrate several very important
points regarding biblical interpretation. First, it is often
unwise to single out isolated verses to establish a principle.
Both of these verses appear in the New Testament, but they
do not appear anywhere near each other or in the same kind
of context. Second, the immediate context must be taken
into account. The first verse above is found in a narrative
portion of Matthew's gospel, describing what Judas did after
feeling remorse for betraying Jesus. It is no more an endorsement of hanging than it is that one should betray others,
especially Jesus. The second verse is Jesus' injunction to the
lawyer after telling him the parable of the good Samaritan.
Third, the reader must be sensitive to how the verses are
being used in the Bible itself, not only whether they
are describing or commanding but whether they are being
applied to particular people or to larger groups, with only
the particular situation or a larger framework in mind.

[1] Except where otherwise stated, Biblical quotations are from the New International Version.

The second passage to examine is Romans 13:1: 'Everyone must submit himself to the governing authorities.' According to this and most other translations, this verse has been understood by many to mean that the State is entitled to unqualified obedience by the Christian. The consequences of this interpretation have been horrific. History is strewn with various tyrants who have demanded allegiance from the Church on the basis of this verse, to the extent that good and sincere Christians have stood by while outrageous acts have been perpetrated. Most Christians today would probably say that this verse does not apply if the government demands immoral actions, but the verses surrounding it do not qualify the verse in that way. The verse goes on to say that God has established the authorities, with the idea that to defy them is to defy God himself. This example is different from the first one cited above. Whereas the two verses above illustrated the difficulty when verses are taken out of context, this passage illustrates that reading the Bible requires close attention to how the individual words are used. The word translated 'governing' is rarely discussed by those commenting upon the verse. The way this word is used elsewhere in the New Testament by Paul seems to indicate that it is a word that does not mean positional superiority or governance but qualitative superiority, and hence, for an authority figure, moral superiority. If this is the proper understanding, then Paul is commanding obedience to morally superior authorities, not to all authorities simply because they are in positions of power.

In the light of these two examples, several more general points regarding biblical interpretation can be drawn out. The first is that one must be careful in what one means by calling something 'biblical'. By 'biblical', one usually means that the Bible in some way – either directly or indirectly – endorses, advocates or approves the thing being spoken of.

Therefore, there is a difference between something being 'in the Bible' and something being 'biblical'. For example, the Bible records many instances of actions labelled sin or evil – such as unjustified killing, sexual immorality, idolatry of various sorts – but these can hardly be called 'biblical' in any meaningful or useful sense. They are in the Bible, to be sure, but they are not advocated or endorsed as patterns for behaviour, even if they are not always overtly condemned when discussed or presented. Furthermore, there are many episodes and events recorded in the Bible on which no comment is made by the biblical writers. For example, there are narratives that record historical events, such as a nation or a people travelling from one place to another. These events are in the Bible but of themselves they cannot be called biblical in the sense that is being discussed. This is not to deny that a biblical writer may interpret these events in a particular way or that a modern interpreter might not see something of significance in the event – for example, something about the way God preserves and protects his people – but the events themselves are not 'biblical'. Lastly, it must be noted that there are all kinds of phenomena that may resemble phenomena in the Bible, but they may not be called 'biblical' just because of what is perceived to be a resemblance. For example, there may well be various religious groups that imitate or induce religious experiences that resemble behaviour manifested in the early Church. Laying aside the issue of how one interprets such phenomena in the biblical context, the superficial similarities say nothing about whether the practices are biblical. They must be evaluated on the basis of a number of criteria, not appearance or similarity alone. Thus from these examples it can be seen that there are various phenomena found in the Bible that cannot be said to be 'biblical'.

In attempting to address these kinds of issues, Coates

makes a distinction between biblical, unbiblical and non-biblical phenomena (Roberts July 1994: 46; cf. Coates November 1994: 24), although he tends to place the manifestations of the Toronto Blessing in the category of non-biblical phenomena. One must be careful with this kind of reasoning. There seems to be some ambiguity within the movement regarding the biblical basis for the phenomena of the Blessing. On the one hand, chapters and articles regularly offer prooftexts designed to establish the biblical foundation. However, there are also explicit and implicit denials of the need for a biblical basis. If the phenomena are categorised as non-biblical, they are potentially placed beyond evaluation on biblical grounds, a foundation that would seem to be important to any group wishing to be thought of as concerned with 'word and spirit'. As Forbes says of treating the phenomena as non-biblical, 'that seems a dangerous conclusion to make and an even more dangerous principle on which to discern things which are happening amongst God's people' (November/December 1994: 13). The argument is sometimes offered that all sorts of modern behaviour could not be justified if a prooftext were required, such as driving automobiles, etc. (cf. Hunter December 1994: 8; Coates November 1994: 24). There are three considerations here. First, isolated prooftexts, as discussed above and to be illustrated below, do not constitute adequate justification for any phenomenon to be considered biblical. Passages must be interpreted in their contexts. Second, claims are nevertheless being made that some of these phenomena are the same as those seen in the Bible. Therefore, they can and should be evaluated in the light of the biblical text to see if there is genuine conformity. Third, as Coates states, 'The Bible is not a text book but a test book. We draw our experiences alongside Scripture to test them to see whether they are of God or not' (November 1994: 24). The discussion below attempts to do just that, on the basis of the explanations offered by the proponents of the Toronto Blessing.

Occasionally proponents of the Toronto Blessing cite numerous biblical examples where people are corrected for being too narrow in their perspective regarding God or where people respond positively to God in various ways (such as worshipping him), and this is used as evidence that the specific phenomena of the Toronto Blessing are therefore biblically justified (Lancaster October 1994: 6–8; Hoffman 1994: 2; Peel August 1994: 3–4). This kind of approach proves nothing of the sort. To use some of the examples sometimes cited, it may be true that Apollos, though knowledgeable, did not know everything about the Spirit (Acts 18:24–26) or that Nicodemus as a teacher of Israel did not know what it meant to be born of water and the Spirit (John 3:4–10) or that Peter found it difficult to abandon his Jewish dietary food laws (Acts 10) or that Stephen's persecutors were resisting the Spirit (Acts 7), and the list could go on, but it says nothing about whether a given contemporary phenomenon is Spirit-generated, and it certainly does not prove that a phenomenon is biblically well-founded because some in the Bible resisted the Spirit and were chastised for it. Each example must be evaluated on its own merits without prejudicing the case by implicitly casting aspersions of spiritual immaturity on those who do not accept. For example, one author states (Monks October 1994: 12): 'When God visited these early Christians with power [Acts 2] – something happened. Similarly, when God moves in power today we can expect something dramatic to happen.' Even if the logic of equating early Church experience and present experience is sound (this is an interpretative decision, to be sure), and even if reactions to the experience are similar (13), it does not follow that what is being seen in churches today are manifestations of the Spirit as found in Acts 2.

This leads to a further important consideration. That is that every reader of the Bible who is concerned to identify a 'biblical' position must work within a framework of interpretation (as Jackson (1994: 297–9) recognizes in one of few discussions of the method of biblical interpretation from within the movement, although theological categories take precedence). This is not the place to enter into discussion of what such a framework entails in all of its specifics, but some cognizance must be taken of the following matters. For example, the Bible was written in several ancient languages, the Old Testament in Hebrew (with a few sections of Aramaic, another ancient Semitic language) and the New Testament in Greek. Hence our English translations are not in fact the actual biblical text but a rendering of it, and hence themselves reflect an element of interpretation. It is best to try to get back to the original languages where possible, for the obvious reasons that it is the canonical text that one is attempting to understand and that its very wording is important. Another factor to recognize is that the Bible is full of various kinds of writings, including poetry, narrative (some historical and some fictional), letters, and the like. Each of these forms of writing demands attention to how best to read it. For example, one does not read the daily papers the same way one reads a letter from a friend. To be more precise, one does not read the tabloids the same way one reads the major papers, or a letter from one's bank manager the same way one reads a letter from one's spouse. What we know to do when reading various kinds of literature in everyday life needs to be realised when reading the Bible as well.

A further factor to consider is the importance of reading in the light of the broader context. The broader context helps to establish whether a given verse or passage is simply part of a conveyance of information, whether it is an injunction addressed to a specific audience or whether it is a statement of more timeless and abiding value, and hence could be normative for the Church today. For example, when Jesus says 'Go and do likewise' (Luke 10:37), his words have immediate application to the lawyer to whom he is speaking. One might well argue on the basis of the context and Jesus' use of parables that these words have wider application to anyone who finds himself or herself in the position of being a neighbour to one in need (this is not to say that we have always done this well). It is a misapplication of the verse to say that it is an injunction simply to go and do anything else.

One of the most important contextual factors to consider, and one often overlooked (perhaps because of our modern English Bibles bound in one cover), is the differences between the Old and New Testaments. Understanding the relationships between the Testaments is highly complex, but whatever one concludes on the issue, the differences between the two must be acknowledged. For example, the Old Testament was the Scriptures for a particular ancient ethnic-religious group, reflecting their encounter with God. The New Testament is the Scriptures particular to the Christian Church. The Christian Church may well have a number of similarities with ancient Israel as God's chosen people, but it also has some distinctive features, including its place in history with regard to the Messiah and the coming of the Holy Spirit, its composition and membership requirements, and its goal and function. Even though the Old Testament was the Bible of the early Church, and was included in its Scriptures, there are numerous places within the New Testament itself that attest to the importance of rightly understanding the Old Testament in relation to the New (e.g. Mat. 5:17–48 and Rom. 10:4–13 in the context of Rom. 9—11). The New Testament must provide the starting point for understanding the Old Testament within the context of the Christian Church. There are many other factors influencing biblical interpretation that could be mentioned – for example, how dependent interpretation often is upon a given church tradition – but these are sufficient to begin to assess the biblical basis of the Toronto Blessing.

The Use of the Bible by the Toronto Blessing

The wider church movement concerned with so-called 'signs and wonders' and related theologies, of which the Toronto Blessing is apparently a part, has generated plenty of controversy regarding its use of the Bible. In this section, I will not engage in a general assessment of this movement. On the one hand, there seem to be a number of serious issues regarding biblical teaching which have been and should continue to be addressed by this movement. These not only relate to so-called spiritual manifestations but to teaching regarding sickness and health, adversity and prosperity, and the like. In the light of the sufferings of Jesus in his life and death, to say nothing of the constant and widespread suffering of the apostles, such as Paul (e.g. 2 Cor. 6:3–10; 11.23–28), it is difficult to find a convincing biblical basis for thinking that Christians are entitled to enjoy continuous good health and prosperity on this earth. On the other hand, I am not attempting to argue that there is a biblical basis for claiming that the so-called charismatic gifts or gifts of the Spirit have ceased. Those who try to make this case (e.g. on the basis of 1 Cor. 13:10 or some construal of 1 Tim. 5:23) seem to me to be stretching the evidence beyond breaking.

This is not to say, however, that all of the manifestations of these gifts are genuine or that all of the practices that attend them can be justified from a biblical standpoint. For example, regarding the so-called gift of tongues in the context of orderly worship, there are manifest phenomena that differ from the passages often cited to justify the practice (1 Cor. 12, 14). The gift of tongues is one of many gifts, seen by Paul not to be either denigrated or given priority, although in relation to prophecy it is apparently not to be preferred. The overall design is for the building up of the Church, hence it is to be done in an orderly way (Paul says by two or three at most, and one at a time), with interpretation, otherwise silence is to be maintained. I realize that there are a number of issues that could be debated here. In establishing a biblical position, one must pay attention to the whole of the biblical text, not picking and choosing the portions one likes, as when speaking in tongues is aggressively promoted at the expense of other gifts, and the issue of women keeping silent in the church, addressed in the same passage, is completely ignored (see Hunter December 1994: 9–10). Sometimes issues of interpretation are not easy, and sometimes one must conclude that the biblical position for something is quite different from what one has been led to believe. One must also avoid disjunctive or either/or thinking, that is, thinking that one must either totally accept or totally reject a position or phenomenon. It may be that one accepts something in theory, but realises that its practice or utilisation is not biblically justified.

Before looking at specific phenomena and biblical passages, it merits noting that there is much that is probably biblically sound with the Toronto Blessing, in so far as it takes seriously traditional orthodox Christian belief regarding the awesome power of God the Father, the person and work of Jesus Christ and his centrality in Christian experience, the role and function of the Holy Spirit as Christ's emissary, and the need for the Christian Church to demonstrate Christ's

love in its treatment of members and the world at large,
to list only a few things. For instance, Chevreau's chapter
'Expanding our Operative Theologies: A Biblical Foundation
for Renewal and Revival' (1994: 37–69) has much that is
unobjectionable, but also not germane to a direct defence of
the Toronto Blessing. Even if all of the above beliefs were
agreed to, it would leave a range of issues still to be discussed
and evaluated in the light of their biblical precedent. My
question is with the particular phenomena that have come
to distinguish the Toronto Blessing as described and practised
by those within the movement.

In analysing the biblical basis for the Toronto Blessing, it
is perhaps best to examine in detail some of the methods
utilised and passages cited in justification of some of the
phenomena. The seriousness of understanding the biblical
passages for those involved in the Blessing is revealed in a 15
June 1994 handout on Ministry Values from Holy Trinity
Brompton, where it says in the context of biblical authority
that the Spirit of God and the Bible, or written word,
never conflict. This sets an appropriate set of priorities for
investigation. The logical conclusion would be that if one
claims that certain phenomena are of the Spirit, but the
Bible shows otherwise, then one cannot claim that the Bible
supports these phenomena as of the Spirit.

To illustrate that there is some room for rethinking the
issues, one can cite how this particular phenomenon is
referred to. At the apparent instigation of the Vineyard
Church in Toronto, this supposed movement of the Spirit is
to be referred to as ' "times of refreshing". . . or renewal
rather than revival', because revival 'has the connotation of
touching the larger community' (Vineyard Church Toronto
1994). This phrase 'time of refreshing' is taken from Acts
3:19 (3:20 in the Greek text) as rendered in many modern

English translations.[2] But this phrase itself raises several interpretative issues, including understanding of the wording of the text and the larger context. The concept of 'refreshing' is defined above by 'renewal' as opposed to 'revival'. A check of the context, however, reveals that this passage is part of a speech by Peter to unrepentant Jews (3:12) rebuking them for their sin regarding the death of Jesus (3:13–17) and calling them to repentance and turning to God (3:19). It seems that on their repentance or conversion depends in some way the 'times of refreshing' and the second coming of Christ, probably seen as one complex event. Thus it is probably inappropriate to link Mark 1:14–15, the announcement of the inauguration of Jesus' ministry, with this 'time' (as Chevreau 1994: 49 does), but more appropriate to link a passage such as Mark 13:30–36, which probably refers to the times surrounding Christ's return. Some would argue further, on the use of the same Greek word in Exodus 8:15 in the Greek translation of the Old Testament, that Peter is speaking of relief from trials and tribulations that are thought to accompany the coming of the Messiah and that were pronounced on unrepentant Israel by Jesus (Mark 8:30). In any case, it is clear that this verse, though perhaps creating a catchy way of talking about the Blessing, may well speak of revival – or at least conversion – at the end of the age, with particular reference to Israel. To take it as a reference to one of several periodic times of renewal in the Church is a misapplication of the passage. If such a crucial conceptual passage is misunderstood perhaps other passages have been misconstrued as well.

In fact, there are several ways in which the phenomena of

[2]e.g. New International Version, New American Standard Bible, Revised Standard Version; but cf. Weymouth's translation with 'seasons of revival', something that the Blessing has not brought: Jackson 1994: 296; Chevreau 1994: 48 translates it as 'times of recovery' [?].

the Toronto Blessing are interpreted that seem to go against sound principles of biblical analysis. The first practice concerns *taking passages out of context*. It has been noted that there have been manifestations of quasi-drunkenness by those evidencing the Toronto Blessing. According to Hoffman (1994: 6), the signs of this spiritual drunkenness are not being able to speak, walk or stand, even by the leaders who try to preach, teach or lead services. Two passages are repeatedly appealed to in defence of this as a manifestation of an outpouring of the Spirit.[3] The first is Acts 2, especially vv. 13–15:

> Some, however, made fun of them [probably the apostles] and said, 'They have had too much wine'. Then Peter stood up with the Eleven, raised his voice and addressed the crowd: 'Fellow Jews and all of you who live in Jerusalem, let me explain this to you; listen carefully to what I say. These men are not drunk, as you suppose. It's only nine in the morning!'

Hoffman concludes from this passage that the believers 'must have been acting like men and women drunk with wine' (1994: 6). After observing that he claims to have seen similar behaviour in church meetings, he concludes that 'The manifestation of being "drunk in the Spirit" in the book of Acts is the same manifestation that we are experiencing today' (p. 7). Jackson is more cautious (1994: 305): 'That the 120 newly filled believers [but cf. v. 14, which indicates instead that it was probably the eleven apostles and Peter] were acting in a "drunken" manner is what is known as an argument from silence.' But he goes on:

[3]Coates November 1994: 25 also cites 1 Sam. 1:13 and 19:24, neither of which is relevant; and Jackson 1994: 305 cites Jer. 23:9, refuted by Forbes November/December 1994: 13.

The text never says that they were but it is obviously inferred. They will not be accused of being drunk because they were speaking in different languages. They would have been accused of such because they were acting like drunks, i.e., laughing, falling, slurred speech by some, boldness through lack of restraint, etc. The analogy of the gift of the Spirit being 'new wine' would lend itself to the connection. (pp. 305–6)

Several observations must be made, however. First, the context in Acts gives no indication that the apostles were acting like people drunk with wine. What the text says is that at the day of Pentecost the apostles were filled with the Holy Spirit and began to speak in tongues or languages. Jews gathered in Jerusalem from the furthest reaches of the dispersion heard their own languages being spoken. There were two reactions to this phenomenon. Some were amazed and perplexed at hearing their own languages being spoken, while others speculated that the speakers had had too much wine. Of course, Peter strongly and clearly denies such a charge. There is no evidence that the apostles were acting in the way described by Hoffman not being able to speak, walk or stand. And it is sheer – and ungrounded – speculation to say that the text 'infers' (Jackson means 'implies') such a conclusion, simply because he thinks that he knows why and in what circumstances one might be accused of drunkenness (with traits that surprisingly resemble those used to describe the Toronto Blessing). On the contrary, the apostles were doing something phenomenal which some *misattributed* to drunkenness. However, Peter quickly refuted this, instead of encouraging it. Second, the reference by Jackson to 'new wine' is confusing. The analogy that he is describing is apparently one whereby the mockers accuse the apostles of having drunk new wine (or better translated sweet wine), and since the Spirit has affected them, the new wine is equated with the Spirit. Even though the Spirit has caused the apostles to react in this way, it is doubtful that the misunderstanding of ridiculing onlookers should be determinative in describing the work of the Spirit.[4] Third, there is no such thing in Acts (or in the New Testament) as being 'drunk in the spirit'. The charge of drunkenness is unfounded speculation by those who are said to be making fun of the apostles. The label of drunkenness is a label of ridicule by onlookers, not a title encouraged by the biblical text. In the light of the above considerations, it is doubtful that what is being experienced by the Toronto Blessing churches is the same as that depicted in the book of Acts.

The second passage regarding quasi-drunkenness is Ephesians 5:18: 'Do not get drunk on wine, which leads to debauchery. Instead, be filled with the Spirit.' In an intriguing defence of quasi-drunkenness, Moss (6 June 1994) first cites John 7:37, where Jesus says that if anyone is thirsty that person should come to him and drink, then moves to Acts 2:15, where Peter says that the apostles are not drunk (see above), and then says that he has seen people behaving like drunks, characterised by him as staggering, slurring their speech, and singing and laughing. Then citing Ephesians 5:18, Moss claims it would be unscriptural to forbid the quasi-drunkenness. There are several problems with this argument. First, the prooftexting of these three passages, linked by the concept of drinking, is akin to the linking of passages cited above. The passage in John is metaphorical, using the analogy of thirst and drinking to speak of belief and receiving of the Spirit. The passage in Acts is an explicit

---

[4] Cf. Matt. 9:17, Mark 2:22, and Luke 5:37–38, where it is said that old wine is to be preferred over new wine because it has had a chance to ferment properly; and John 2:10.

denial of drunkenness. The passage in Ephesians demands closer attention.

In Ephesians 5:18, Paul is contrasting drunkenness, linked with debauchery or dissipation, with the filling of the Spirit. Scholars vary in their understanding of the background to Paul's statements, including possibly misconduct in the church, a contrast between foolishness and wise behaviour, believers who despair at life in this present age and hence get drunk, or participation in pagan religious practices. In any case, Paul is repudiating the practice of drunkenness. Paul is *not* saying (as some in the Toronto Blessing seem to be implying) 'don't get drunk with wine but get drunk with the Spirit'; he is saying not to get drunk with wine but *do be filled* with the Spirit. This is consistent with other Pauline passages on drunkenness, such as Romans 13:13, where drunkenness is included among other forms of immorality, and 1 Thessalonians 5:6–8. The consequences in Ephesians of being filled with the Spirit must be noted. They are not those of falling down, slurring one's speech and the like, but 'speaking to one another in psalms and hymns and spiritual songs, singing and making melody in your heart to the Lord, giving thanks always for all things to God the Father in the name of our Lord Jesus Christ' (Eph. 5.19–20 New King James Version).

Second, it simply cannot logically follow from Paul's rejection of what is probably actual drunkenness by Ephesian Christians that this can be considered a biblical practice that would be unscriptural to forbid. It simply does not follow that a clear denial of a practice, because it is recounted in the Bible, becomes a scriptural basis for it. Third, Jackson looks to the same tenses of the Greek verbs of command to argue for an analogy between being drunk and being filled with the Spirit (1994: 306). The linkage is apparently valid, in that alcohol often played a role in ancient religious practice and ancient writers such as Philo noted similarities in outward manifestations of drunkenness and religious experience. What we must take note of in this verse is Paul's denial of the one and endorsement of the other. Jackson concludes that 'While there is not much to go on here, the two NT passages [Acts 2:13ff.; Eph. 5:8ff.] are important texts. The possibility of being "drunk" in the Spirit is consonant with the overall flow of biblical precedent' (306). This is a strange conclusion to reach. There is no such concept of being 'drunk in the Spirit' in the Bible, since there is no biblical precedent, the two passages in fact denying an equation of the work of the Spirit with drunkenness. This faulty logic is to confuse things mentioned in the Bible with being biblical. As noted above, there are many things mentioned in the Bible that cannot be considered biblical. Drunkenness (or quasi-drunkenness) appears to be one of them.

The second practice concerns *misconstruing a concept*. Uncontrollable laughter has been one of the major hallmarks of the Toronto Blessing. Although some admit that the signs of laughter and tears are different signs from those experienced by the early Church (Monks October 1994: 12), others have tried to justify the phenomena as biblically defensible. For example, regarding laughter, Psalm 126 is often cited, especially v. 2 (e.g. Jackson 1994: 307; Coates November 1994: 27). As Hill (September/October 1994: 10) points out, however, this is one of few examples of laughter in the Bible 'being an expression of joy'. But the context makes it difficult to accept this passage as normative for contemporary church practice, since it is a commemoration of God's deliverance of the captives from Babylon back to Zion. More is needed than simply the fact that some of those returning laughed. Coates (November 1994: 27) cites Psalms 2:4 and 37:13, but these are examples of God laughing at and deriding his enemies, hardly suitable to justify the

Toronto Blessing's displays of laughter, especially if laughter is to be equated with joy. The concept is apparently being misconstrued.

Contending that he has found many passages that speak of people being joyful, laughing and being glad, Hoffman (1994: 7) cites a number of passages mentioning joy and/or gladness: Isaiah 9:3; 56:7; 51:3; Psalms 16:11; 25:6; 45:7; Nehemiah 8:10; Hebrews 1:9; and especially Acts 13:52. In interpreting what being 'filled with joy and the Holy Spirit' (Acts 13:52) means, he asks, 'Is it really so far fetched to believe that the disciples, as they were filled with the joy of the Lord, at times broke out in spontaneous and perhaps uncontrollable laughter?' (7; Jackson 1994: 308 argues similarly). Several issues are raised by this. First, the issue is not whether one thinks that something is or is not too far fetched to believe. What one should be concerned with is the biblical basis for uncontrollable laughter, and this argument based on speculation seems inadequate to make the case. Second, even if it could be shown that the disciples did at times break out in laughter (but it has not), this does not mean that what they were doing should be normative for today's Church. Neither does it mean that what goes on in Toronto Blessing churches is a true manifestation of the Spirit. These connections remain unproven. Third, if I were concerned to define joy in the New Testament (it is common to try to extrapolate from joy to laughter – but this has not been proved), I would first note that often there is an uncomfortable equation of Christian joy with adversity, not with uproarious laughter. Consider James 1:2–3: 'Consider it pure joy, my brothers, whenever you face trials of many kinds, because you know that the testing of your faith develops perseverance', or Philippians 2:17–18: 'But even if I am being poured out like a drink offering on the sacrifice and service coming from your faith, I am glad and rejoice with all of you. So you too should be glad and rejoice with me', and many other similar passages (e.g. 2 Cor. 7:4–7; 1 Pet. 1:8; cf. v. 6). Thus Jackson's conclusion based upon three verses (Ps. 126: 2; Ecclus. 3:4; John 17:13) that 'laughter fits within the general flow of Scripture' (1994: 308) is apparently unjustified.

The third practice concerns *misapplying a parallel*. For example, in several recent justifications of trembling and shaking, the following verses are cited: Jeremiah 5:22; 23:9; Psalms 2:11; 99:1; 114:7; Habakkuk 3:16; Acts 7:32 with reference to Moses in Exodus 3; and Daniel 10:8–10. This looks on the surface like convincing evidence that the trembling and shaking evident in Toronto Blessing churches are biblical. But such an acceptance is questionable for several reasons. There is the serious question whether the trembling and shaking are the same thing and occur in contexts at all similar. It is not enough that the English translations use these words; the contexts must be analysed. For example, in Jeremiah 5:22 God is commanding an unrepentant Judah – characterised as 'foolish and senseless' (v. 21) – to repent because they do not fear him and his awesome power. In Psalm 2:11, the words are addressed to the kings and rulers of the earth, so that they might not be destroyed. In Habakkuk 3:16, the prophet in his prayer to God quakes at the destructive power of God in anticipation of his destruction of his enemies. In Daniel 8:8–11, Daniel is responding to a vision that caused others to flee. It is undeniable that the Bible records incidents of trembling and shaking before God, but these supposedly parallel passages are being misapplied in that they are taken as justification of similar phenomena supposedly witnessed in Toronto Blessing churches. One author (Jackson 1994: 304) cites three of what he considers New Testament examples of biblical precedent for shaking: Matthew 28:4: 'the guards . . . shook and became like dead men', Acts 4:31: 'the place where they were meeting was shaken', and James 2:19: 'Even the demons believe that — and shudder'. Interesting as these examples may be, they are completely irrelevant for establishing a precedent for bodily shaking as an indication of reception of the Holy Spirit by a person. Only slightly better is Philippians 2:12 (Coates November 1994: 24), where Paul tells Philippian Christians to 'work out your salvation with fear and trembling', hardly a context reflecting the Spirit's coming upon a person.

The same kind of misapplication seems to be occurring when discussing falling over or being slain in the Spirit (e.g. Hoffman 1994: 4–5). First, equating falling over with being slain in the Spirit is potentially misleading. The one implies a natural process and the other a post-Pentecost experience, the kind of experience supposedly being described in the literature regarding the Toronto Blessing. To equate the two would seem to require further definition. Second, Hoffman admits that many of the passages referred to could merely indicate falling out of respect or awe, or because the person was terrified (4). After these kinds of passages are eliminated, he still thinks that 2 Chronicles 5:4, Ezekiel 1:28, 3:23, 44:4 and especially Daniel 10:8–10 are germane. Third, if what is being defined by Hoffman is being slain in the Spirit, a post-Pentecost experience, then the examples cited above apparently do not apply. If they do, they raise the question of what it means to have an outpouring of the Spirit and what distinguishes the Toronto Blessing. Fourth, several passages are still cited from the New Testament, Matthew 17:6, Revelation 1:17, John 18:6 and Acts 9:1–8 (cf. 22:4–11 and 26:12–18). None is germane to the Toronto Blessing, however. In the first, the disciples fall face down before the transfigured Jesus, but Jesus immediately tells them in v. 7 to 'get up'. The second involves a phenomenal vision of the son of man enthroned in heaven, and the third is a response by those coming to arrest Jesus in the actual physical presence of Jesus himself. The fourth with its parallels is the conversion of Paul. Jackson (1994: 301, mis-cited as 9:22–6) interprets this last episode as indicating that 'falling was a normal response to a divine visitation'. However there are several problems with this example and its interpretation. First, one must be cautious in using Paul as normative for Christian experience. His life before his conversion, his life after his conversion, and his conversion itself are anything but representative of normative Christianity. Hence it is difficult to single out a single episode or part of an episode and say that this characterises a normal Christian experience. Second, this raises the question of what is meant by 'normal'. Does this mean simply that an experience is one of several possible and not impossible responses to being in the divine presence? This would seem to be the sense needed for Acts 9:4, 7, where it is noted that Paul fell but his travelling companions stood there, having heard the sound but not seeing anyone (but cf. Acts 26:14). But a stronger sense of 'normal' would apparently be needed for advocates of the Toronto Blessing to justify the widespread and frequent instances of falling down. But this raises the further question of why so few examples can be mustered from the New Testament. If 'normal' means frequent or usual, then why is it that John 18:6 stands out as a response to Jesus, and why are there not hundreds of passages indicating that virtually every time people see Jesus they fall on the ground in the presence of the Divine? In other words, regardless of whether people fall down in the Bible (and they do, for a variety of reasons, many of them quite natural causes), the evidence of post-Pentecost being slain in the Spirit, especially in terms of how it is understood by the Toronto Blessing, is apparently slender indeed.

A recent account that I heard reported spoke not only of

humans making animal noises (see below on roaring) but of animals speaking audibly in human voices. So far as I know, these reports are unsubstantiated in any credible way, but for the sake of argument, it is worth considering where such a claim may have come from. The precedent for animals speaking like and to humans appears to be based upon the parallel of Balaam's donkey speaking to the prophet (Num. 22:28–30). But there are several problems that indicate that this is a misapplication of a supposed parallel. First, the context is completely different. The donkey spoke because it was being beaten by Balaam for not proceeding in the direction he intended, since the way was being blocked by an angel. The donkey does not testify, but merely questions Balaam's cruelty, and then does not speak again once Balaam understands the reason for the donkey's recalcitrance. Apart from the speaking of an animal, there is little else in common with these supposed incidents. It appears that a biblical event has been seized upon to attempt to justify (or create?) some phenomenon as biblical. This single incident in the Bible does not provide such justification.

The fourth practice concerns simply *interpreting a passage incorrectly.* Concerning the 'roaring lion' phenomenon, this has been defended by reference to Hosea 11:10–11: 'They will follow the Lord; he will roar like a lion. When he roars, his children will come trembling from the west. They will come trembling like birds from Egypt, like doves from Assyria.' Mary Pytches says that the roar is 'a prophetic roar . . . and the children are beginning to gather. The prodigals are coming home. Things are happening' (Roberts October 1994: 3). Several points are worth mentioning. First, this is a passage in an Old Testament prophet and its immediate context is in terms of a rebellious ancient Israel. Second, one must note that God is the aggressive figure, with Israel depicted as trembling children following him. Third and most important, it is not the children who are roaring but God. Several exegetical difficulties must be overcome before this verse can provide a biblical basis for human roaring, including understanding and application of prophecy specifically given to Israel as being relevant to the Church. More difficult to overcome is that Israel's depiction as penitent children seems to be in terms of their being caught in their sins, although they may not be fully penitent. In Hosea 13:7–8, when Israel is depicted as continuing to sin, God is depicted as a lion, a leopard and a bear, attacking and tearing sinful Israel to pieces. Most difficult is the simple fact that there is no justification in the passage cited for those who experience God's blessing (if they can be equated with Israel) to be roaring. This is a misinterpretation of the passage. If anything, they should be like birds and doves. This does not mean that cooing is commended, but that they should be like animals afraid before an awesome beast.

Are Important Biblical Concepts Being Overlooked?

Some may resist the conclusion towards which this discussion seems to be moving, that there is no firm biblical basis for the phenomena of the Toronto Blessing. Two forms of argument are available to them. The first is that the Bible is not the full extent of Christian revelation. Evidence for this may be sought in instances of contemporary prophecy, words of knowledge, etc. As I noted above, a number of those involved in the Blessing recognise what this implies and want to maintain that any practice must be tested against Scripture. This is not the place to discuss this issue, but those who would attribute the same level of authority as the Bible to these supposed revelations have accepted some concept of an open canon, perhaps without realising it. The vast mainstream of orthodox Christianity throughout most of its history has held to the concept of a closed canon. I would argue that this was for good reasons. The alternative is a canon with flexible boundaries, subject to expansion (and potentially subtraction). But a set of logical and theological questions are raised by this. How does one judge which new revelations should be included? What happens if a new revelation contradicts previous revelation? Should the old revelation be discarded or do we introduce blatant contradiction into the Scriptures, and how do we decide which one to follow in future circumstances? What does this imply about the traditional concept of God and his knowledge and power? If the new revelation introduces only material that supports previous revelation, why is this revelation necessary? It is reassuring to see that most of those writing on the Toronto Blessing are not heading down this path.

The second form of argument is to appeal to the complexities of the Acts of the Apostles. For example, Chevreau states (1994: 62), 'When the Book of Acts is reviewed, it is incontestable that there is a remarkable diversity of charismatic spiritual experience represented in the early communities, and that it is so rich in its variety that it defies standardization, form and formula, and sometimes even interpretation!' It is true that the book of Acts has remarkable diversity in it, but this should make one very cautious in drawing upon it to establish normative Christian behaviour for today. One can, however, occasionally be overwhelmed by the diversity and fail to see the patterns of regularity, sometimes because they are too expected or because we do not want to see them. For example, in Acts there are at least seven important occasions that typify the successful spread of the Gospel under the Spirit's direction: Acts 2, Pentecost; 8:9–24, the conversion of Samaritans, including Simon the Sorcerer; 8:26–40, the conversion of the Ethiopian Eunuch by Philip; 9:1–19, the conversion of Paul (cf. also 22:4–16); 10:1–48, the conversion of Cornelius by Peter; 16:16–40, the conversion of the Philippian jailer; and 19:1–7, the coming of the Spirit to Ephesus. I have not mentioned Paul's first missionary journey in Acts 13—14, where he is expelled, flees, or is stoned in Pisidian Antioch, Iconium and Lystra, or Acts 17, where there are riots and other troubles in Thessalonica and Berea. Even if these are included, there are several common patterns to mention. Although there are a number of more spectacular manifestations of the Spirit such as tongues, healings and the like recorded in these accounts (though they are certainly not found in the vast majority of the episodes), the one common factor that unites all of them together is a clear proclamation of the Gospel. It would appear that any Toronto Blessing church wanting to be faithful to Acts would make a clear proclamation of the Gospel – that is, the saving efficacy of the death and resurrection of Jesus Christ – absolutely central. The second most common factor, to be found in the seven 'successful' evangelistic efforts but not in the prematurely curtailed visitations of Acts 13—14 and 17, is the occurrence of water baptism (I would argue this is even the case in Acts 19:5, for example, where it just mentions baptism). In an effort to analyse the spectacular, one must not overlook the mundane. If one follows the logic of the Toronto Blessing, one could well argue that if proclamation of the Gospel and water baptism are the two unifying factors in the Acts account, then these ought to be the phenomena present at most if not all services. That there is concern in at least one Toronto Blessing church over this matter is evidenced by what I heard a minister say on the occasion of a baptism. He preached a sermon in which he fervently reminded his congregation of the importance of baptism and expressed the strong desire that they would restore it to its appropriate place, one that had been lost in the spectacular events of the preceding year.

Conclusion

Perhaps the words of someone writing from within the charismatic renewal movement in a charismatic publication are a fitting way to conclude (although I do not agree with everything said):

> It is a common error to believe that Christians who are filled with the Holy Spirit cannot be deceived. In fact, *those who have been baptised in the Spirit are more likely to be deceived* than conservative evangelical or traditional, orthodox believers, who have had no such experience.
>
> The reason for this is that the latter judge right and wrong by the use of their intellect, or reason. They form a judgment based upon principle, rather than upon experience or emotional reaction. The more believers are soaked in the Word of God, the more likely they are to be able to make a sound judgment.
>
> Those who are in the greatest danger are believers who have been newly baptised in the Holy Spirit and who lack maturity in the Word of God. They have opened their lives to the manifestations of the Spirit and they begin to judge all things on an experiential, rather than a rational, basis. If they lack a depth of sound teaching in the Word, they are an easy target for the enemy. (Hill September/October 1994: 11–12; emphasis his)

This chapter has tried to look at much of the supposed biblical foundation for the phenomena of the Blessing. In the light of a recent conclusion reached by the Board of the Associated Vineyard Churches, that 'Rather than promoting, displaying or focusing on phenomena, we want to focus on the main/plain issues of Scripture' and that 'If [critics] can prove to us by sound exegesis and logic that we are wrong, we will change' (Hunter December 1994: 8, 9), it is hoped that this chapter will aid in discussing the biblical basis – or lack of it – for the phenomena of the Toronto Blessing.

Bibliography

Chevreau, G. (1994) *Catch the Fire: the Toronto Blessing, an experience of renewal and revival*, London: Marshall Pickering.

Coates, G. (November 1994) ' "Toronto" and Scripture', *Renewal 222*, 24–25, 27.

Coggins, J. R. and Hiebert, P. G. (eds.) (1989) *Wonders and the Word: an examination of issues raised by John Wimber and the Vineyard Movement*, Winnipeg, MB: Kindred.

Forbes, D. (November/December 1994) 'Is There a Biblical Basis for the "Toronto Blessing"?', *Prophecy Today 10*, no. 6, 12–13.

Hill, C. (September/October 1994) 'Toronto Blessing – True or False?', *Prophecy Today, 10*, no. 5, 10–13.

Hoffman, D. (1994) 'Renewal Manifestations: a *biblical* look at 5 manifestations of the Holy Spirit', Toronto, ON: Mantle of Praise Ministries.

Holy Trinity Brompton (15 June 1994) 'Ministry Values', Holy Trinity Brompton, Brompton Road, London SW7 1JA.

Hunter, T. (December 1994) 'The Vineyard Synod grasps the nettle', *Alpha* Magazine Prayer and Revival Supplement, 8–10.

Jackson, B. (1994) 'What in the World is Happening to Us?: a biblical perspective', in P. Dixon, *Signs of Revival*, Eastbourne: Kingsway, 295–330.

Lancaster, J. (October 1994) 'This is No Laughing Matter', *Directions 65*, 6–8.

Monks, R. (October 1994) 'What is This?', *Directions 65*, 12–13.

Moss, N. (6 June 1994) 'This is what was spoken by the prophet Joel, Acts 2:16', Queen's Road Church, Wimbledon.

Peel, J. (August 1994) 'How are we to respond to current worldwide events in the Church?', Vine Church.

Roberts, D. (July 1994) 'Rumours of Revival', *Alpha* Magazine, 25–27, 46.

Roberts, D. (August 1994) 'Revival Call', *Alpha* Magazine, 14–15, 17.

Roberts, D. (October 1994) 'Calver Speaks Out', *Alpha* Magazine Prayer and Revival Supplement, 3.

Vineyard Church Toronto (20 April 1994) 'Suggested Ministry Tips', Vineyard Church Toronto, Toronto, ON.

3

Risen with Healing in his Wings

An Exploration of the Psychology of the Toronto Blessing

ROYSE MURPHY

I saw that God's longing takes three forms but all have the same object. (The same is true of us too, in the manner of longing and object alike.) The first is his longing to teach us to know and love him more and more — which both suits and helps us. The second is his longing to have us share in his blessedness, like souls who have been taken out of suffering into heaven. The third is to fill us full of bliss — this will happen on the Last Day, when we shall be filled full to everlasting.

Julian of Norwich 1373 (tr. 1966: 195)

To disregard the human need for the experience of God's love, or the need for worth in God's eyes, is to pass over the more fundamental aspects of pastoral ministry. It is possible in a crisis to explore great areas of meaning but fail to respond to an individual's need for recognition and affirmation. There is little doubt that people, even the most 'normal' of people, experience crisis at the end of the twentieth century: crisis in relationships, crisis in the economy, in unemployment, in the relevance of faith, and in the expression of faith. There is a sense of powerlessness in crisis, a need for the perfect touch of the Divine in the midst of despair.

When the manifestations of the Toronto Blessing were reported in the press in 1994, criticism was directed at the extreme form of utterances and behaviour. They were described as superficial and immature. Comparisons were made to mass hysteria or a cathartic therapy known as 'Primal Scream'. Doubts were expressed whether the manifestations were of the Spirit or not. Some commentators were convinced intuitively that the Spirit is at work in Renewal of the Church, some were intellectually convinced that excessive emotional expression in belief precludes any substance on rational grounds alone. However many Christians preferred to use both emotional and rational exploration in order to judge the phenomenon.

There is a natural tendency to assume that those who write about psychology and religion are doing so out of a need to discard or 'debunk' faith. It is certainly true that science, and psychology in particular, has been used to do this in the past. However it is also self-evident that if God created the universe and all that is in it, God also created the human need to understand physical and psychological processes and indeed the processes themselves. Many Christians have found, in their understanding of human need, a basis for a deepening faith. From my own experience both in ministry, and in general practice and psychiatry, I have found it increasingly inappropriate to regard distinctions between psychological and spiritual processes as clear-cut and exclusive. However, in exploring the Toronto Blessing, it is important to understand the needs and expectations of those who receive the Blessing and the role of the spiritual leader, and to begin to understand why the manifestations are not universal. Also, if there are instances where an outcome may be unhealthy, we must ask why this is so.

The Individual Experience

Other chapters have detailed the manifestations themselves, and it is clear that the features of religious experience are repeated in succeeding ages. Writers from William James to Gerald Priestland have drawn our attention to similarities of experience across a range of individuals and, to some extent, across a range of world faiths. While experience is a feature of conversion to belief, it is also a feature of living and growing insight into faith, and is in that sense universal to believers. Experience is also a feature of healing in the broadest sense — that is physical, emotional and spiritual healing, not only the removal of physical disease. For healing, like conversion, is not usually a once-for-all experience. In the words of the baptism service we traditionally say that we 'turn to Christ' and that turning to Christ continues through life. In the context of the Toronto Blessing, which is seen as primarily a renewal experience, experiences of healing and conversion also seem to have occurred. Are the people who experience renewal and healing 'neurotic' or in some way abnormal, or do they differ from others only in the way they experience spiritual insight?

The conclusions that Alister Hardy drew from eight years of collected accounts concurred with William James' view in 1902 that a religious experience arose out of a real human discontent resolved by a real intervention by God. He also concluded that the power of prayer was important, and feelings of security, worth and happiness are associated with such experience (Spilka 1985: 155).

While illness and adversity may be the precursor of religious experience, moments of joy and happiness, or even being in a place of beauty may be of significance. It is not possible to generalise to a statement that the need for a spiritual experience of God always arises out of neurosis, difficulty or guilt.

Gerald Priestland broadcast a series of programmes titled *The Case against God* in 1984, in which he undertook a lengthy series of interviews. As many as 60 per cent of the population are reported to have experiences which could be defined as religious, although many would not choose to define them that way (Priestland 1984). So a majority of people may base their beliefs substantially upon mystical experiences of God rather than rational thought. Alister Hardy's research featured in the programmes, as did the question 'Is religious experience simply wish-fulfilment?' For some people mystical experiences have been so real that rational examination is inappropriate; but for others the reality of life and human imperfection generate a scepticism by which they have dismissed spiritual experiences entirely. For if the mystical experience of God, in particular the ecstatic experience, has no real connection with God then faith, even in a Creator, has no personal element. It makes no difference to our lives; it may even be self-deception.

Traditionally, Christians have redefined the adversity and imperfection of human existence as a series of opportunities for transformation through faith for both persons and society. The evidence for such transformation is objective, whereas the experience of God is not. How is the Christian then to discern whether psychological circumstances determine the experience, or whether the outcome is a response of the Holy Spirit to that need?

The leaders of the Blessing movement have recognised the dangers of open and chaotic worship. In some cases people have been asked to reduce noise in order to allow the Spirit to speak (Roberts 1994: 157). The discernment applied to the Blessing that it should bear fruit is clearly relevant, as is the observation that for some people the experience becomes more important than any other aspect of their Christian growth. However, the majority of the people who experience the Blessing report that as well as the benefit of the experience they have noticed improvements in their lives (Chevreau 1994: 212).

These reports would suggest that it is the Blessing itself that has brought about this change. Ecstatic experience is not, however, the only way in which insight may be gained into one's faith. Study, reflection, prayer, interaction with other people, and traditions and ritual in worship have always been perceived as beneficial to faith. Why is it, then, that some find the ecstatic experience of greater benefit than other ways of seeking God's strength?

Perhaps our personality may influence the way in which we appreciate and grow in faith. The observations of Jung on personality types revealed that there were differences in the way in which people assimilated experience, and related to the outside world and each other. We primarily use 'thinking' or 'feeling', or 'intuition' or 'sensation', expressed in an extraverted or introverted way, and although we are not excluded from other modes of expression, we prefer the familiar and may find the unfamiliar frightening or alien (Jung 1971: 450). Jung's concepts were subsequently developed into the 'Myers–Briggs' psychological theory of spirituality which is widely used today (Goldsmith 1994: 12). Ecstatic experience may be the preferred means of relating to God for those who have an extraverted, feeling and sensation-based psychology, whereas for thinkers the rational approach is preferred, and for introverted intuitives meditation and reflection may be of greatest benefit. Interestingly, some leaders who have been deeply influenced by, and who have 'carried with them' to other groups the Blessing, have not had the experience themselves.

One consequence of Jung's exploration of our spiritual

selves is that the lesser used spiritual expression may hold the greatest power for crisis, fear and change (Goldsmith 1994: 82). So for instance, an introverted thinker (while rejecting absolutely the subjective) may, through deeper spiritual need, have an unexpected ecstatic experience which may be of a deeply converting nature. It may be, quite literally, the last thing that they ever intended to do. An explanation is that, because of the preferred personality type, emotional reactions to events in a person's life have been forcibly stored away (or 'repressed') to emerge later in crisis as an unrecognised need (Bryant 1987: 21).

In one publication, *Renewal Manifestations* by David Hoffman of California, those critics who feel that the ecstatic laughter associated with the Blessing cannot be of the Holy Spirit in turn have the criticism levelled against them that their 'spiritual grid' may be wrong (Hoffman 1994: 8). The concept of a spiritual grid, because of insights gained in the models of Jung and Myers-Briggs, is clearly of relevance to the whole psychological issue of individual spiritual experience. However it seems to me unnecessarily arrogant to dismiss those for whom a different mode of spiritual experience and expression is more relevant.

It is also of interest that the Blessing has arisen (as have other charismatic manifestations in the past) at a time when levels of individual and social stress, and a disillusionment with society, have affected large numbers of people. Of relevance also is the way in which religious expression and understanding (especially in the tradition of the longer-established churches) have fallen into disuse by the majority of the population; while at the same time a general belief in God persists, even among the young. When the accepted social language and values exclude religious belief in favour of technology and self-promotion, the only way in which people can explore their spiritual needs may be within the context of disinhibition and emotional outpouring. There are clearly parallels to the need to have a 'rave' experience; and if the impulse is strong enough a 'rave' experience can be achieved without the need for drugs.

In *The Go-Between God*, written in 1972, John Taylor saw in the charismatic manifestations an individual need; a true but negative causative factor at work:

> They are a passionate expression of self–concern. Need is met. Unconscious tensions are released. Loneliness is appeased. Sickness is healed. Uncertainties about the future are resolved. Inarticulate weakness finds rich self–expression.

This self–centredness, which the experience tends to emphasise, runs counter to the purpose of religion to put self at the service of others. On the other hand he saw in the experience a bringing together of rational intellect and spontaneous intuition, aspects of the human life so easily separated from one another (Taylor 1972: 220).

For many critics of the Blessing, such extreme forms of charismatic expression are simply hysterical outbursts that have nothing to do with genuine Christian spiritual growth. Some clergy, including George Carey, are asking whether the experience leads to a superficial experience, or whether the congregations are indeed exploring their Christianity in the context of the realities of life, and the practical demands that are put upon faith. The issue of neurosis has been extensively rejected by the leaders of the movement and by researchers who have looked at the personalities of participants. A large number of participants who experienced ecstatic phenomena at a John Wimber conference in 1986 were interviewed by David Lewis, and found to have a variety of personalities. Only 12 per cent ranked as highly extrovert and neurotic, and he asserted that the majority were not likely to be suggestible or hysterical (Lewis 1994). A criticism by the psychologist Dr Dorothy Rowe, quoted in the *Daily Mail*, that the manifestations were due simply to the release of adrenalin within a socially contagious atmosphere has been rejected by Evangelical leaders who have asserted that the majority of participants have been normal individuals with a real experience of God's renewing presence (Roberts 1994: 44).

The link between religious experience and psychological illness is not entirely clear. Unfortunately, such a link has not been tested objectively. The literature suffers from a prejudice that religious conviction and experience is in itself evidence of psychological instability. If the observation that a majority of people in the rational late twentieth century have had religious experiences is accurate, then assumptions that it is a sign of illness are clearly incorrect! There is evidence that suggestibility and mystical experience may be related, but also that psychological well-being and openness to experience may associate strongly with religious experience. As Spilka and others point out, the human experience of being prepared to 'surrender' oneself to an experience of God can only narrowly be interpreted as psychological 'weakness' (Spilka 1985: 192).

For the person for whom the ecstatic experience is the preferred path to God, for the rationalist for whom it is an unexpected experience, or for the person for whom the experience is in reality an aspect of an illness, our pastoral response must be to understand the ground in which the experience has grown and to give appropriate guidance and help. The leaders themselves have recognised that the manifestations may not always be of the Spirit, and have been careful to include in ministry teams only those who have been closely associated with the charismatic work of the Church. This may protect against unhealthy ecstatic

expression, but it may also influence the manifestations themselves.

The Group Effect

It is significant that the phenomena associated with the Blessing occur in meetings within the context of worship rather
than as individual experiences. The experience is highly
individual and personal, and a participant typically reports
being absorbed and washed over by the Holy Spirit, sometimes to the exclusion of everything else, for long periods
of time. What is the nature of the communal worship which
enables the Blessing to occur?

Research suggests that in the church non-attender and in
the frequent attender there is a high degree of mystical
experience. The non-attender seems to regard the Church
as irrelevant to spiritual experience and may find that the
doctrines of the Church conflict with this very individual
experience. The infrequent attender has a low level of mystical experience; however the frequent attender, perhaps
because of the doctrinally acceptable character of their
experiences or because their local church is accepting or
even encouraging of the experience, has a higher level of
spiritual experience (Spilka 1985: 186). The group is influential in the experience of the individual. Other situations
in which a group effect has been observed suggest that there
is a tendency for the group to make decisions which were
more 'risky' than an individual member of this group would
have made (Argyle 1967: 254). This occurs because risky
behaviour is valued in that group and cautious individuals
move to a more extreme position after group discussion.
Under some conditions, individuals behave in a disinhibited
fashion in large groups (Argyle 1967: 167). Whether extreme
behaviour in groups is due to added confidence, selective

communication (unusual suggestions creating interest) or the psychologically disinhibiting effect of numbers, its relevance to charismatic worship should be noted.

It is also of interest that some participants who experience the Blessing may return to be ministered to on many occasions, perhaps to the exclusion of other forms of spiritual growth. This attachment to the experience is of concern, not just on the grounds of superficiality but because it may represent an escape from psychological trauma rather than a resolution of such trauma. The 'rave' experience is a real disinhibition without foundation in reality and with no lasting benefit. On the other hand, participants may be finding a safe place emotionally to discharge accumulated anxiety and trauma in a cathartic way and therefore be open to real insight and spiritual growth. Dr Rowe's observations are relevant: the question is whether the emotional outpouring results from an experience of the Holy Spirit or simply from anxiety or need, and whether it is healthy or unhealthy psychologically and spiritually. Experiments reported in 1962 showed that people who were artificially aroused emotionally by stimulant adrenalin could be influenced in a group into interpreting their feeling as anger or as euphoria by the presence of planted 'stooges' (Spilka 1985: 157). Participants can be influenced by suggestion in a group even when as individuals they are not in objective terms 'suggestible'. It is therefore quite possible that leaders of ecstatic worship can influence the interpretation of the experience of the participants. Children are particularly suggestible and tend to copy their parents: how much more powerful is the group experience for them?

Although the mainstream churches have been slow to make a judgement about the Blessing, some conclusions can be derived from published material. In *We Believe in the Holy Spirit*, published by the Doctrine Commission of the Church of England, charismatic gifts are recognised as genuine scriptural and historical features of the Christian faith. Concern is expressed, however, that there is a

> subtle group pressure towards constant joy, with perhaps insufficient awareness of psychological typecasting. The confidence and outgoingness which may be natural to the extrovert (and the insensitive) should not necessarily be viewed as the certain marks of 'victorious living'. The ebulliant characteristic of some charismatics may be inappropriate in many lives for internal or external reasons; it may even desert those who have it, when they are under stress, or physical pain, or clinical depression. If the dominant model of Christian daily living and spirituality which those persons encounter is one of continuous euphoria, then the actual Christian fellowship which is supposed to be supportive and therapeutic not only feels uncaring and judgemental to the sufferers, but also inevitably makes any depression worse. (Doctrine Commission 1991: 54)

Canon John Young is quite clear in his view that the Blessing is not entirely of the Spirit:

> Get a group of people together, create a sense of expectancy, make suggestions about likely behaviour, clear a large space, move among them, and something like this is likely to happen. . . . People are suggestible. We are not observing the work of the devil, though the leaders would be wise not to put too much stress on roaring like a lion. Nor is this – as some leaders claim – a great outpouring of God's Spirit in revival. It is a movement which fits well into our secular and superstitious age which will believe pretty well anything, from energy pyramids to laughing in the Spirit. (Dixon 1994: 230)

Dr Patrick Dixon, in a very comprehensive review of the

current charismatic scene, gives strength to the view that certain kinds of group experience may be psychological in origin. He writes:

> My own view is that we are not witnessing brainwashing on a grand scale . . . nor mass hysteria. We are, however, witnessing what happens when a large number of people experience an altered state of consciousness at the same time, as part of a profound spiritual experience.
>
> Clearly, as we have seen, other factors may be operating in some people, including copy-cat behaviour, exhibitionism and spiritual conflicts of various kinds. However, my own observations lead me to conclude that a great many manifestations are due to this other effect, related to prayer, the work of the Holy Spirit and other factors all working together in a group setting. (Dixon 1994: 258–9)

However, Patrick Dixon believes that altered states of consciousness, which can be induced by euphoria, anxiety, suggestion, or hyperventilation (as well as a number of other factors of focused worship), can bring the participant to an awareness of God; but it does not necessarily bring him or her into the presence of God. Emotion is part of every relationship we have, including our relationship with God. If the movement is a genuine revival, he argues, the evidence will not be seen merely in the manifestations (which may have a very large psychological component) but in an altered attitude to life and to other people (Dixon 1994: 276–9).

Leadership

Traditional evangelical worship has usually involved high profile charismatic leadership with highly directive skills and teaching. However the leaders believe, rightly, that the power rests with God, and that human attempts to lead the Church into new areas are by their very nature likely to be flawed and to bring difficulty (Roberts 1994: 154). In addition, there have in recent years been examples of television evangelists who have been taken up with the personal power of leadership and consequently fallen from grace. The congregation responds enthusiastically to their leadership, and so the leaders involved in the Blessing movement have tried to avoid a high profile, even by changing the name of one organisation to remove the personal element from the leadership, and have avoided describing the phenomena directly to their congregations.

It seems unlikely, however, that members of charismatic and Evangelical churches could have remained unaware of the powerful emotional expression of the Blessing and its reported benefits. In addition, congregations that have charismatic and trusted leaders would be confident in the presence of these leaders to allow themselves the spiritual experience. It is in the nature of human beings, however much they hold to democracy and individual belief, that they identify leaders who will enable desirable change to happen (Argyle 1967: 173). It is also the role of those leaders to serve the needs of the people they represent in guiding and achieving such change. I would be concerned if the leaders of the Blessing movement did not take their leadership seriously enough to recognise their role in its propagation. It is not objectively relevant to this argument whether the Blessing is always of the Spirit or not; the evidence is that leadership is traditionally and psychologically essential to the Church; and that a denial of this is naive and potentially irresponsible.

In other contexts, for instance in the Encounter movement of group therapy in the sixties and seventies, adverse effects were noted where the leaders were aggressive and challenging. Paradoxically, groups in which a high level of challenge was experienced also produced rapid and useful change for some participants. In general, however, a 'safe' group in which learning and change could occur was one in which the leadership was energising, responsible, and caring. Where the leadership was *laissez-faire* or irresponsible, controlling or impersonal, negative effects including psychiatric illness were noted (Lieberman 1973: 251, 256).

Leaders of encounter psychotherapy groups in the sixties were keen to enable groups to be 'leaderless'. One advocate was Carl Rogers who aimed to lead a group with 'unconditional positive regard', with genuineness and empathy, in order to allow genuine feelings to be expressed (Whiteley 1979: 150). Although his expressed aim was to allow the group to run itself, analysis of his gestures and non-verbal interventions showed that he continued to have a large controlling influence on the group, perhaps because of the group's high level of regard for him and its need for leadership.

While understanding the charismatic leaders' expressed wish to allow the Holy Spirit to be free to work within worship settings in which the Blessing occurs, I would be surprised if they did not, in fact, have a high degree of control over the proceedings, albeit from a very low-key standpoint. Dave Roberts in *The Toronto Blessing* reports that the leader is able to bring considerable order into the service at will where an apparently unruly and intrusive element has crept into the manifestations: for instance when the noise and chaos is so great that no ministering can proceed without interruption. He refers to disorder and 'spiritual anarchy' which the wise pastor should take steps to control (Roberts 1994: 154–7).

In the 'Suggested Ministry Tips' of the Toronto Vineyard Church, those who minister to participants are directed to look for 'those who are most obviously anointed'. People who do not manifest anything unusual when they receive prayer are encouraged to remember that God works differently in different people. 'Remember to encourage people that it's not manifestations we are after but changed hearts.' Later, however, in the 'Tips for Praying for People' it says 'If no manifestation of the Holy Spirit comes within a few minutes, it is often wise to simply allow that person to "soak" and come back later' (Dixon 1994: 325). Although the intention is to emphasise a broad basis for the reception of the Blessing, it is clear that those who manifest an obvious 'anointing' will receive prayer and ministry from the leaders. It is probable, then, if people come to receive the Holy Spirit at such a meeting that they would be disappointed not to merit the affirming prayer of the leaders, the 'experts' in the Holy Spirit, who are paying attention to those who fall.

Could this lead to heightened anxiety or a feeling of exclusion which might result in either the repetition of the observed phenomenon through suggestion, or in some cases the simulation of the phenomenon? It would be wrong to assert that this occurs, but important to recognise that there can be pressure on an individual to respond, caused by their own expectations and needs, within a group who also expect manifestations to occur. It is difficult for a leader to pay attention to all who need healing equally; but an advantage of healing services without manifestations of the Spirit is that nothing is expected of an individual by a group, and nothing is expected of the Spirit but a real and healing presence for that individual in his or her need. Our Christian understanding of God is that grace can be given to us in every aspect of our lives regardless of our merit and need; and all that is asked of us is that we are willing to receive it.

It is also possible that a person who has a limited experience of Christianity might believe that the Blessing is the exclusive sign that the recipient is accepted not only by the ministry team, but also by the Church and by God; and that the absence of the Blessing is a sign that they are rejected by God. This might be particularly true for children who have very little understanding (especially in the late twentieth century) of the traditional building blocks of faith. It is therefore important that the evangelical leader also gives credence to less dramatic expressions of faith. The whole Church may indeed need also to review its pastoral care and teaching to those who have experienced dramatic manifestations. It is clearly unhelpful, and in many cases inaccurate, to dismiss all ecstatic experience as emotional hysteria. On the other hand all cases should be considered in their spiritual and emotional context, so that any real emotional difficulty will not be overlooked.

In some cases the Blessing reveals difficulties which the ministering team deduce to be demonic possession. If such a diagnosis is made intuitively about a participant whose emotional and spiritual history is unknown to the ministry team there may be a hasty and premature decision that deliverance is required. In the case of serious mental illness, such as psychosis, deliverance may simply effect a reinforcement of the individual's beliefs, not a release from them.

As far as I am aware there has been no increase in religious mania or other associated psychotic illness as a result of the Blessing, though it seems possible that in some cases disinhibition could produce serious emotional difficulty in the short term which an enthusiastic or naive ministry team might have difficulty in handling safely.

Implications for Pastoral Care

At the beginning of this chapter, I drew attention to the needs of ministers with pastoral concerns for those who experience the Blessing and their concern to understand as far as possible participants' needs and expectations. I hope that, in this brief review of the possible psychological mechanisms involved in our seeking after a forgiving and loving God, some of the difficulties and pitfalls may have been explored. My concern is that some individuals (perhaps a minority) may have deep psychological problems which require careful counselling and which can be addressed only by careful and broadminded assessment and follow-up. Individuals may come to ecstatic services with real needs for acceptance and self-worth which are not fully satisfied. I have concerns that the teaching at the services should be about the broad spiritual experience and love of God; not just confined to the ecstatic experience. This is not to say that all who have needs must be ill – we clearly all have needs and we are not all ill! It would help if religious experience in all its forms was better accepted by the more established denominations; though this also is a problem of interaction between personality, experience, and rational thought. The possibility that the participant's main motive is disinhibition rather than spiritual growth would be another area of concern, and a ministry team could draw some conclusion about this through adequate interview.

The group effect cannot easily be ignored. The Holy Spirit works for individuals, and most historical visionaries have had solitary experiences. The Blessing, in contrast, occurs in groups, and in groups with accepted and trusted leaders. It is difficult to deny the possibility of a group effect. I have deliberately avoided the terms 'mass hysteria' and 'peer pressure' because they carry unhelpful pejorative implications. On the other hand, it is naive to assume that group effects do not occur in the context of the Blessing and similar experiences. In my opinion leaders need to be aware and judge objectively how these effects may help to power the Blessing within congregations. Whether or not the Holy Spirit is always behind the manifestations, ecstatic phenomena always have some emotional precedent or context. It is the unexpressed need which requires attention, not the manifestation itself. The literature suggests that leaders in most cases are aware that this is so.

I am also concerned that the individual does not regard the Blessing as a sign of being accepted into the group. This is an unintentional form of peer pressure that may be happening in some cases. Our acceptance into the body of Christ is through informed faith and baptism, and both of these need rational deliberation as well as an emotional and spiritual conversion to belief.

Lastly, I am concerned about the attitude and understanding of ministry teams at services. There must be an appreciation of why participants come for the experience and of what they expect to happen. Also, why do some people need to receive the Blessing so many times? Is spiritual insight denied them in any other form? Ministry teams should ask themselves if they are selective in their ministry. For God's love is for all, regardless of need or merit.

Leaders should not underestimate the power of their leadership. Even if they lead in a low-key fashion, they are identified as holding power, and can influence the mood of a congregation with the least of remarks. Leadership is approved by and needed in human society. In the context of church life it should be always enacted in partnership with the Holy Spirit; and it is naive to assume that leadership can have no role at all.

Julian of Norwich believed that we shall be filled with bliss on the Last Day; indeed our present experience will always be an imperfect one. It may be that the spiritual renewal of the Toronto Blessing will continue to spread through Christian congregations. However, we need to remember that our imperfection is not removed by belief; and that our human nature (both in its positive and negative aspects) will always affect our interaction with God, and our interpretation of God's will for us.

Bibliography

Argyle, Michael (1967) *The Psychology of Interpersonal Behaviour*, Harmondsworth: Pelican.

Bryant, Christopher (1987) *Depth Psychology and Religious Belief*, London: Darton, Longman and Todd.

Chevreau, Guy (1994) *Catch the Fire*, London: Marshall Pickering.

Dixon, Patrick (1994) *Signs of Revival*, Eastbourne: Kingsway.

The Doctrine Commission (1991) *We Believe in the Holy Spirit*, London: Church House Publishing.

Goldsmith, Malcolm (1994) *Knowing Me Knowing God*, London: Triangle.

Hoffman, David (1994) *Renewal Manifestations*, Toronto: Mantle of Praise Ministries.

Julian of Norwich (1966 tr. Wolters, Clifton) *Revelations of Divine Love*, Harmondsworth: Penguin.

Jung, Carl G. (1971) *Psychological Types*, London: Routledge and Kegan Paul.

Leiberman, Morton A. *et al.* (1973) *Encounter Groups: first facts*, New York: Basic Books Ltd.

Lewis, David (1994) 'Trots and Wobbles', *Christian Herald* 15 October 1994.

Priestland, Gerald (broadcast from 28 October 1984) 'The Case against God', British Broadcasting Company, Radio 4.

Roberts, Dave (1994) *The Toronto Blessing*, Eastbourne: Kingsway.

Spilka, B. *et al.* (1985) *The Psychology of Religion*, Englewood Cliffs, NJ: Prentice-Hall.

Taylor, John (1972) *The Go-Between God*, London: SCM Press.

Whiteley, J. Stuart and Gordon, John (1979) *Group Approaches in Psychiatry*, London: Routledge & Kegan Paul.

4

Have We Been Here Before?
A Historian Looks at the Toronto Blessing

JOHN KENT

The Toronto Blessing, the phenomena of people falling over, laughing and weeping, in a kind of religious ecstasy, which is said to have affected a variety of more or less 'evangelical' churches in Britain, and the claims made for its orthodoxy and importance, look familiar to the historian who has done work on Protestant revivalism and similar movements in other contexts. There is the characteristic revivalist assertion that something new and successful is being done by God at this very moment, and the further claim that this allegedly supernatural activity should be accepted by the mainline churches because it is in line with what has happened in the past. References are usually made to the biblical 'speaking with tongues' which is mentioned in Acts and the Pauline Epistles, and to the religious phenomena associated with eighteenth and nineteenth-century revivals of the Protestant Evangelical kind, those identified with George Whitefield and the Wesleys in Britain, and those connected with the Americans, Jonathan Edwards (1703–1758) and Charles Finney (1792–1875). These eighteenth and nineteenth-century revivals are seen as bringing about the renewal of true Christianity in an alien, fallen world. As Francis Mac-Nutt says, for example: 'Along with the wild behaviour [i.e. physical reactions to alleged supernatural stimulus] came new life, while the established churches tended to ossify in their pews' (MacNutt 1990/94: 97). These revivals are also described as having counteracted the danger of 'enlightenment rationalism', a favourite target of modern Christian apologetic and equally distrusted in the Vatican of Pope John Paul II. The influence of the 'Enlightenment' is said to have produced dead orthodoxy or downright heresy in the Christian churches and to have left no room for the direct intervention of the Spirit of God. Some evangelical leaders now say that the alleged revival which centres on the Toronto Blessing stands in this positive, central tradition.

The most important part of this case is the claim that the 'Evangelical Revivals' have been the life-giving essence of modern Christianity. This could be put more diplomatically than MacNutt puts it, but the underlying assertion is widely accepted in the Evangelical sub-culture, and in much British church-historical writing. There emerges a quasi-Hegelian theory of human history, in which the sinfulness of humanity is opposed by the activity of the divine Spirit, and although it is arguable that the Spirit has made little observable progress, especially in the twentieth century, there remains the comfort of the assurance that at the End of History the Spirit will prove to have overcome Sin in such a way that contemplation of the whole process will reconcile the redeemed to the past history of creation. Themes of this kind belong to the philosophy of history as much as to theology. It is natural that Christian theologians and historians should want to insist that both in the present and in the future God is in control of human history – why else should one trust the ethical and spiritual guidance either of God himself or of his representatives on earth? It is not absolutely unreasonable to believe that in the longer run the universe makes sense; it is a big jump from this very broad statement to the claim that the Protestant Evangelical tradition of revival is the cutting-edge of this supernatural oversight. One has also to account for the resurgence of Roman Catholicism after its eighteenth-century debacle, and the way in which the twentieth-century West has been steadily penetrated by non-Christian religious institutions. On a more secular level, historians are not bound to accept the optimistic eschatology of contemporary Christian theology as a way of looking at the past. They may have an obligation to report the state of the Christian philosophy of history, but they are also free to ask for the grounds on which its more detailed assertions are based. They may ask, for example, how far it makes sense to compress the activities which can be loosely called 'the eighteenth-century Enlightenment' into a single, pernicious force which is said to have corrupted both the secular and the religious institutions of the past two hundred years.

In any case, the recent collapse of the Anglo-Catholic party in the Church of England should remind us that many of the judgements which sustain the interpretative framework of 'church history' at the moment need to be re-examined. In view of the long-term failure of Anglo-Catholicism to remodel Anglicanism in terms of its own ambiguous understanding of 'tradition', and its inability to prevent the Anglican ordination of women priests, the history of Victorian Anglicanism has to be given a new context, in which the role of Anglo-Catholicism and the career of John Henry Newman may look more tragic than transforming. Similarly, one needs to look again at the importance which has been assigned to the Evangelical revivals in the history of modern Christianity, and especially in the history of Protestantism. It is true that at the beginning of the eighteenth century the very existence of Protestantism, as Professor W.

R. Ward, for example, has demonstrated effectively in some
of the essays which he collected in *Faith and Faction* (1993),
was critically challenged in Europe, including England. The
Baroque form of Roman Catholicism, as much political as
religious, was greatly weakened as time went on by the
predominance of the political interest, but nevertheless
seemed round about 1700 to be tightening its grip on an
opponent (and one should not pretend that Protestantism
was not an opponent) which lacked the will to survive.

Equally, there is no doubt that by the end of the Napo-
leonic Wars Protestantism had recovered to a remarkable
extent. The traditional explanation of the change hardly goes
beyond saying that the Evangelical revivals happened, and
that their deeper origin was supernatural. From the historian's point of view this is inadequate. A large part of the
explanation of the specifically Protestant renewal can be
found at a secular level. On the one hand, the Roman
Catholic Church had discovered in the French Revolution
how weak its grasp was on the secular order in Europe, and
just how deep ran civil resentment against the traditional
form of its institutions. On the other, Prussia, as the instru-
ment of the Hohenzollern dynasty, became an aggressive
and also Protestant power, bent on reorganising Germany
politically in its own material interests, and on reducing the
authority of the Catholic Habsburgs. Neither the Stuarts nor
Roman Catholicism were restored to power in Britain, a
political fact which had become obvious by 1745, while
Britain itself, also under a rising German dynasty, gave Protestant culture a potentially vast new power-base by the com-
pletion of the conquest of North America. In their turn the
political and economic strength of the United States and
Britain would rapidly enable Protestant missionary societies
to compete with Catholic missionary orders in much of the
extra-European world. The Protestant crisis of the 1690s had

ended for the time being, but the Protestant churches had benefited far more from the direction of economic, social and political change than they had from the first and second Great Awakenings in America and from the increase of Wesleyanism in Britain. And although the political nationalism which developed in Britain from the 1750s relished the use of religious symbols and celebrated the divine mission which God had allegedly bestowed on the Protestant British, neither this nationalism, nor the equivalent Roman Catholic style of French nationalism, brought much credit to Christianity.

Evangelical historians prefer to see the revivalist tradition as acting successfully against secular economic and political trends. They often make the kind of claim which one finds repeated by, for example, Dave Roberts (1994: 45), that 'many would argue that Methodist revivalism helped prevent atheistic French-style political radicalism engulf Britain in the eighteenth century'. There are non-Evangelical sources for this idea, but Elie Halévy, the French scholar who was one of the first professional historians to take Wesleyanism seriously, and the late Edward Thompson (the brilliant but not always convincing author of *The Making of the English Working Class*, 1963), both believed, though on different political and ideological grounds, that there *ought* to have been a revolution in England at some point between 1789 and 1848. Halévy could not understand why Britain had not been more violently affected by the French Revolution, and Thompson, a romantic marxist, could not understand the relative passivity of the British proletariat in the first half of the nineteenth century. In the effort to explain why their particular revolutions had not happened, they both paid too little attention to the strength and determination of the essentially secular ruling élites in Britain at this time, and overstressed the importance of the slow advance of respectability and religion in the middle regions of society. In fact, there was no revolution because the British state was quite powerful enough to prevent one. No doubt the Revival, as Professor Ward sometimes calls it, thinking in European and American terms of the period from about 1680 to the 1740s, or Protestant Evangelicalism, if you prefer it, played a part in a Protestant recovery which itself proved vital to the healthy survival of Christianity, but the shift of political and economic power, and the self-confidence which this gave to the ruling élites in Britain right down to 1945, did more for that Protestant renewal than the growth of Evangelicalism, nor should one over-identify the interests of Christianity with the Evangelical tradition.

The historian may press this argument further in the sphere of religion itself. After all, the far from unfamiliar reference to 'atheistic French-style political radicalism' which I have quoted above is another form of modern Western Christianity's fashionable rejection of the 'Enlightenment', a rejection which is above all coloured by the knowledge that one longer-term consequence of the French Revolution was the loss during the nineteenth century of most of the directly political power of the Christian churches, Catholic as well as Protestant. The rise of the 'Religious' (for which read 'Protestant Fundamentalist') Right in the United States since the 1970s shows how unreconciled some parts of Christianity are to the loss of civil authority. The leadership of many national churches, Catholic, Orthodox and Protestant, would still like to be part of a regime in which they could enforce through legislation whatever ethical code, and whatever educational system, they, as a religious subculture, identify with the interests of their nation and of Christianity itself. It is ironical that in some countries democratic forms of government have made it possible once more to seek to impose 'Christian' ethics.

Criticism of the 'Enlightenment', however, also obscures
the much more important point that, whatever the contribution of Evangelical Revivalism to the eighteenth and nineteenth-century survival, not only of Protestantism, but of
Christianity itself as a significant part of Western culture, at
least as much was owed to the ability of liberal but
religiously-minded intellectuals, the vast majority of them
Protestants, who understood how drastically the Enlightenment had transformed all questions of authority, including
biblical authority. Liberal theologians tried to mediate
between the churches, on the one hand, and the rapidly
changing nature not only of science and philosophy, but also
of European society, on the other. The effect of liberal
theology on the churches as institutions was much slower
than the effect on individual theologians and religious
writers, because these corporate bodies were usually tightly
controlled by comparatively small bodies of masculine pastors
and priests. But in the modern world Christianity cannot
live significantly on a diet of existential subjectivism alone,
whether the 'revivals', the glossolalia and the healings are
Catholic or Protestant. Populist Christianity has already
become to some extent a part of the entertainment industry
which is the major component of contemporary Western
culture. American Evangelicalism is beginning to suspect as
much. Mark A. Noll, for example, who is Professor of
Christian Thought at Wheaton College in Illinois, has just
published a significant book called *The Scandal of the Evangelical Mind*, in which he asks: 'Can a christian mind develop
out of American evangelicalism?' and answers that 'based
solely on twentieth-century historical precedent, it does not
seem likely' (Noll 1994: 241); the same question was treated
with equal seriousness but greater skill in Rudolph Nelson's
book, *The Making and Unmaking of an Evangelical Mind* (1987),
a devastating intellectual biography of Edward Carnell

(1919–1967), at one time President of Fuller Theological Seminary in Pasadena, California.

In general, then, the historian of modern Christianity is unlikely to agree that Protestantism has lasted into the late twentieth century chiefly because the divine Spirit has again and again stirred up revivals of the 'Toronto Blessing' type in its ranks. Protestantism owed much to the chances of war, to the needs of politics, and to social and economic changes which released the energy of Protestant countries like Britain. Above all, however, Protestantism prospered because from the eighteenth century onwards a succession of liberal theologians refused the option of appealing to the infallibility of the Church, however that infallibility has been presented.

Moving on now to the further claims made by devotees of the Toronto Blessing that this is in line with what has happened in the past, especially in the eighteenth and nineteenth-century Protestant revivals; what evidence is there for this case? Francis MacNutt, in his book *Overcome by the Spirit* (1994), cites the *Journal* of John Wesley for 1 January 1739: 'About three in the morning, as we were continuing instant in prayer, the power of God came mightily upon us, insomuch that many cried out for exceeding joy, and many fell to the ground.' Later, on 28 July 1762 at Limerick, Wesley reports that 'All were in floods of tears: they trembled, they cried, they prayed, they roared aloud; all of them lying on the ground.' Wesley's *Journal* of 1772 reports that John Wesley asked God to show his power to a 'backslider', James Watson: 'Down dropped James Watson like a stone' (5 June). Bishop David Pytches, in his 1994 prologue to MacNutt's book, draws the conclusion that we have been here before and that 'there are well-known historical precedents for the phenomenon from the revivals of Whitfield and John Wesley, among others' (MacNutt 1994: 2). Dave Roberts, in his book on the Blessing (Roberts 1994), cites the precedents of the 1859

Ulster revival, eighteenth-century Welsh revival, Jonathan Edwards and the eighteenth-century American 'Great Awakening', and the revivalism of Charles Finney in early nineteenth-century America and later in Britain. Roberts suggests that John Weir, writing about the 1859 Ulster revival, 'might well have been speaking of Holy Trinity Brompton, not the parishes of Ballymena and Coleraine' when he describes 'the convulsing of the whole frame, the trembling of every joint, intense burning of the heart, and complete prostration of strength' (Roberts 1994: 119). Guy Chevreau in his book *Catch the Fire* suggests that the Toronto Blessing is 'a well-travelled path' (ch. 4). He focuses on the writings of Jonathan Edwards and concludes that 'many who have been to the Airport [Toronto] meetings will find their personal experiences mirrored in [these] accounts' (Chevreau 1994: 90). Chevreau points out that expressions such as ' "took away my bodily strength", "overbear my body", and "fainting" ', found in Edwards's reports, 'seem to be eighteenth-century equivalents to the falling, resting and "slain" experiences witnessed at the Airport Vineyard' (Chevreau 1994: 77).

If the historian is also asked to comment on the claims that are made about continuity between late twentieth-century and much older religious activity, including Protestant revivalism, he has to look at the cultural context of what is described, in order to understand, as far as possible, why these events in particular have 'religious' significance attached to them, and whether 'religious' seems to have the same meaning in, for example, an eighteenth-century Wesleyan revival as it might have now in a given Christian group like the Vineyard. In other words, one asks to what extent like is being compared with like, and to what extent any comparison is possible at all. One can re-enact past events and rituals, for example, but one cannot recreate them.

One can set up a Greek temple-building, for instance, with its outside altar and inner statue, and solemnly sacrifice a bull. There is enough information, especially on ancient vase-painting, to make this possible. But one cannot experience what the Greeks experienced in their religious exercises, because the world-view in which their experience was contained is no longer available to us, however much we may try the power of a sympathetic imagination. The twentieth-century participant in a reconstructed Greek religious festival would interpret whatever he might experience in such a performance through a contemporary Western outlook. He would, with the best will in the world, be unable to have a Greek religious experience. Similarly, eighteenth-century religious events in Europe took place in a very different cultural context from our own, and in the case of Wesleyanism one is often dealing with virtually unknown citizens of eighteenth-century Britain. It is far from clear that in the early stages of the Wesleyan movement, the 1740s — vital because this was the time when Wesleyanism took off — either John or Charles Wesley understood what effect they were having on those who listened to them, as distinct, that is, from their conscious view of what their intentions were; nor was the Wesleyanism that came out of the eighteenth century exactly what the Wesleys had wanted to establish.

We can look at such problems in more detail in the case of Elizabeth Downs, who was sharing in the activities of the Wesleyan society in Bristol in April 1742, and who exhibited physical phenomena that a modern observer might associate with those of today's Toronto Blessing. Nothing is known about her apart from the 'testimonial' which she prepared for Charles Wesley and dated 13 April 1742. The full text of her description of her religious condition is to be found in *Reformation and Revival in Eighteenth-Century Bristol* (Barry 1994: 85–91). Kenneth Morgan is the editor of this particular contribution. When John Wesley came to Bristol in 1739 Elizabeth Downs was already, according to her account, someone who heard preaching and attended communion: it is unclear whether she was Anglican or Dissenting. Wesley's preaching at first made her feel that if she died as she was she would be damned; in this state of conviction of sin she appealed to Charles Wesley but according to her own account got no satisfaction from him. She went to her Wesleyan Band-leader, Sister Rawlins. The Bands met once a week, had less than half-a-dozen members, and were single-sexed; the Leader was responsible for the immediate spiritual care of this small group. Rawlins said that in reality Downs was receiving frequent offers of divine grace but that she was refusing to believe that they were meant for her. 'She said I would not let God work with me but keep him out of my soul through my unbelief' (86). On the following Sunday Downs was listening to the preaching of a Mr Diaper, and saw Christ, 'evidently by faith . . . with his Blood running from his wounds in Branches Down his arm his body in Great paleness and his mouth as gasping his Last Breath' (87). In the course of the hymn which followed, her heart fluttered as though it would have torn itself out of her body: 'I seemed as though I had been convulsed. My mouth was filled with prayer and praise as fast as I could utter. From thence I believed I was justified' (87). However, the Lord allowed her to fall into doubt. About nine weeks after this experience, John Wesley returned to Bristol from London, and soon after he began to speak she felt her heart 'Clipt as though an hand Graspt it. The stronger he was in power the stronger I felt my pain. At last it Extorted strong groans from me. I was not able to sit but laid myself on the floor.' She thought that she was dying but resigned herself into the hands of God. 'But as soon as Mr Wesley had done I found I was somewhat released but it Left a Great soreness in my heart' (87). After further uncertainty she went to a Band meeting, where she had a vision of Christ 'with his garment as white as snow and a glittering belt about his paps: Sir, it was no formed imagination. I know the father did with love reveal his son' (88). After this she had a clear sense of her justification for at least a fortnight. She had a third vision – 'caught as it were out of the body' (89) – in which she saw Jesus holding a crown out to her and then a sheet of white paper on which she could see no writing. Downs then gives two instances when she had lost the sense of justification, once when reading the journal of William Seward, who changed from being a Wesleyan to supporting Whitefield's Calvinism, and again when she had quarrelled with some one who lived in the same house as she did. She had recovered listening to a Mr Humphreys, who also inclined to Calvinism and would help to start Welsh Calvinistic Methodism in 1743. She felt for a few moments as though her soul was taken into another region. Nevertheless, she points out that 'I cannot be particular but I think it was that time only I received power under Mr Humphreys to receive any promise by faith' (90). As soon as John Wesley returned from London, however, 'I felt the Gospel reach my heart Continually. Great workings and strong strugglings for many months Even to this Day' (90).

It is obvious, I think, that in the Bristol Wesleyanism of the 1740s great pressure was being applied to individuals, especially because of the steady contrast between the states of salvation and damnation in revival preaching and pastoral relationships, not least those of the Bands. This was not, however, purely Protestant, for the stress on eternal punishment was just as strong in eighteenth-century Roman Catholic revivalism. I think that in the late twentieth century we can no longer easily understand as normal this existential state of anxiety about future divine praise or punishment.

Although justification by faith was said to be enough for
salvation, in the early Wesleyan system the certainty that one
was living in a justified state was easily lost because justification itself was so often interpreted by examining the state
of one's consciousness. As Elizabeth Downs's story suggests,
this meant that the ordinary lapses of daily life into irritation
or into doctrinal disagreement (as in the Seward case) were
enough to destroy this sense of being accepted by a divine
power: one fell from grace as swiftly as one fell into ecstasy
or vision. Elizabeth Downs's physical phenomena, as for
example when she had to lie on the floor when John Wesley
was preaching, are usually associated with the absence of this
proper sense of being justified; she lay down because of
the emotional weight of self-rejection developing in her
personality, not because she was experiencing some kind of
self-release, as may be part of the point in the 'Toronto'
meetings. At the same time, the Wesleyan stress on the
freedom of the individual's will meant that the Wesleyan
revivalist soul was always stressed, because the justified
believer had to take some responsibility for what happened,
was always choosing between the way of life and the way of
death. This also helps to explain the bitter controversy, which
intrudes briefly into Elizabeth Downs's memorial, between
John Wesley, determined to have a religious society of his
own, and the Calvinist preachers, led by George Whitefield,
who, perhaps unconsciously, used the doctrine of election
to protect their followers from so much anxiety.

It is too simple, then, to compare physical symptoms with
physical symptoms and then assume that one is talking about
the same religious situation. I don't imagine for a moment
that one can share Elizabeth Downs's total experience of
religion-in-life, or understand why she has these vivid images
of Jesus, once in pain and once in glory, which reassure her
about her future state. The blank sheet of white paper might

be supposed to stand for a charge-sheet from which Jesus had removed all her sins, though she herself was obviously dubious about its meaning, because she added, apologetically, 'as to mentioning this it consisteth not but upon your desiring me to be particular' (89). One can only use language to point towards where differences between the past and the present may lie, without being sure of their content. Here again one has also to remind oneself of the parallels in the Roman Catholic subculture, which was accustomed to visions, though on a more varied pattern.

The existence of pressure, however, in the Wesleyan subculture of the 1740s cannot be denied. It can be illustrated by referring to the kind of letter which Charles Wesley was writing to his brother about conversion at this time. In October 1740, for example, he wrote that he knows how to deal with a justified person who has relaxed the pressure on himself and 'by his past graces [is] strengthening himself in his present wickedness, whether of heart or life' (Baker 1982: 81). Charles says that he would not tell such a person that he had never been justified, but that he was now in a worse state than he was before he was justified, worse even than a gross Pharisee, 'inasmuch as he is now a subtle, inward, spiritual Pharisee, and trusts in the abuse of mercy. Out of this hold I would drive and thrust him down into the deep of his sin and misery' (81). And he added: 'I cannot but think that we agree in the general that everyone who is settled but not on Christ should be unsettled again' (81).

Neither of the Wesleys disowned the physical symptoms which sometimes appeared under the pressure which they put on; they probably recognised that physical responses were an integral part of the religious personality which they were encouraging; that one could not, for the moment at least, have the one without sometimes having the other. In any case, both brothers valued the ecstatic states into which groups sometimes seemed to fall in the course of intense prayer and singing, and thought that these occasions were evidence of the presence of the Divine Spirit. They differed in the long run on the aim of their revival. Charles Wesley's objective remained the reform of the early eighteenth-century Church of England, a reform which would have made the parish priests more efficient religiously and the laity more amenable to the social and moral discipline of the Church as a part of the Hanoverian state. The revivals, with or without physical symptoms, were a means and not an end. He never entirely agreed that the Wesleyan societies should have a distinct organisation, ministry and internal system of discipline. He thought that Dissent was socially divisive, and that Wesleyanism should not become an additional, powerful Dissenting group of churches. John Wesley, on the other hand, put the societies first, and the long-term effect of his work was to weaken the Anglican Church in the nineteenth century. The presence of some physical symptoms in the culture of the 'Toronto Blessing', not in themselves dissimilar from what sometimes occurred in both Britain and North America in the eighteenth and early nineteenth centuries, hardly seems to justify more than a very limited parallel. The energy which was generated in Wesleyanism owed little to visions or more physical reactions to religious and personal pressures. Wesleyanism was a major Protestant event. It had a profound influence on the development of the United States in the nineteenth century and never resembled very closely the kind of religious behaviour which is now concentrated in the American 'Religious Right'. In Britain, Wesleyanism was not as fundamentally important as it became in nineteenth-century America, and its continuity vanished in the upheavals of 1849–57, but the massed forces of Victorian Methodism gave Nonconformity a social weight which it would never otherwise have had.

Finally, there remains the problem for the historian of what people want from religion, as distinct from what the theologian thinks that they ought to want. I think that the historian may posit an underlying popular demand for kinds of ecstasy, whether 'spiritual' or 'material', and whether obtained through drugs or doctrine. With or without ecstatic states, there may be additional demands for healing, personal success (however defined, but frequently financial), other types of request for 'divine intervention', national triumphs and so on. This level of popular demand, which I suspect does not change much from century to century, though it may have become slightly more sophisticated in the course of time, may operate through what we normally call superstition and magic, but it may also interact with the religious doctrine, 'liturgy' and institutions of a specific time and place. These attitudes have no inevitable connection with the kind of existential religious experience that the Wesleys, for example, were pursuing. Popular religion, defined in this way, is as likely to be Roman Catholic as Protestant, and does not have to be Christian at all. The eighteenth-century revivals succeeded partly because they sometimes offered healing as well as doctrine, visions (whether of Jesus or Mary or one of the saints) as well as moral discipline, ecstatic chaos as well as organisation for mutual support, social as well as spiritual. The historian has to examine the way in which this took place in the eighteenth century, for example, as well as in the twentieth century.

What is immediately evident, however, is the mixed nature of religious phenomena. This is not a question of reductionism. In an eighteenth-century society in which the poorer classes had little useful medical treatment available to them; in which their futures were virtually unprotected against the uncertainty of employment and the virtual certainty that old age, if they survived so long, would mean illness and poverty;

in which their education still presented them with a view of the universe in which diabolical forces were rampant and in which a very rigid social system was taken for granted; and in which women were usually not supposed to have anything like a public, as against a domestic, personality, it is no more surprising that what I have called the popular demand on religion should be for health, wealth and happiness, than that in present-day England the setting-up of a national lottery in a crudely materialistic society should prove enormously popular. The lottery, after all, is bound to deliver its big prize to someone every week. It was the interaction of these demands with the more sophisticated moral and doctrinal attitudes of some of the revivalists (though the differences can be exaggerated) which made the eighteenth-century revivals numerically successful, and helped to add to the general religious picture the physical reactions which alarmed some contemporaries. It is worth remembering, however, that when British philosophers like David Hume discussed (and dismissed) what were regarded then as bizarre phenomena, they commonly referred, not to the British revivalists, but to the trances of the French Prophets, as they were called, who fled from Catholic persecution to England at the beginning of the eighteenth century and whom John Wesley encountered in the early days of his own movement, or to the alleged miracles at the tomb of a dead Parisian Jansenist cleric in the 1720s. In fact, when one considers the overall pattern of the eighteenth-century British revivals, the influence on the general public of physical phenomena, similar in kind though different in historical context to those which have distinguished the 'Toronto Blessing', seems to have been slight. They were regarded as ambiguous, rather than decisive. Evangelical revivalism in England in the eighteenth century depended far more on the individual's conviction that he or she had direct, subjective evidence of supernatural power.

Bibliography

Baker, F. ed. (1982) *The Works of John Wesley, vol. 26: Letters 11 1740–55*, Oxford: Clarendon Press.

Barry, J. and Morgan, K. eds (1994) *Reformation and Revival in Eighteenth-Century Bristol*, Bristol: Bristol Record Society's Publications, *45*, 85–91.

Chevreau, G. (1994) *Catch the Fire: the Toronto Blessing, an experience of renewal and revival*, London: Marshall Pickering.

MacNutt, F. (1990/94) *Overcome by the Spirit*, Guildford: Eagle.

Nelson, R. (1987) *The Making and Unmaking of an Evangelical Mind*, Cambridge: Cambridge University Press.

Noll, M. A. (1994) *The Scandal of the Evangelical Mind*, Leicester: Inter-Varsity Press.

Roberts, D. (1994) *The Toronto Blessing*, Eastbourne: Kingsway.

Thompson, E. P. (1963) *The Making of the English Working Class*, London: Gollancz.

Ward, W. R. ed. (1993) *Faith and Faction*, London: Epworth Press.

5
The Worship of the Toronto Blessing?

WENDY J. PORTER

The Concept of Worship

Setting the Framework for Worship

The churches of the Toronto Blessing herald themselves as 'word and spirit' churches, that is, churches where the word is as important as the manifestations of the Spirit (see ch. 2 on the biblical basis of the Toronto Blessing). Therefore, it would seem reasonable in discussing the subject of worship, that Toronto Blessing churches would be concerned to exemplify a worship that is biblically based, and allows for the proper expression of the gifts of the Spirit. They have said as much – but is this in fact the case? In order to decide, perhaps there is a need to begin with establishing fundamental precepts regarding the biblical basis of Christian worship. But with all the books and articles that have been written in recent years on the subject of worship, is there a possibility of addressing the issue in a few pages? There is no space to refer to something like Peterson's (1992) detailed study of biblical words translated into English as 'worship', but there is still one significant factor that can be singled out and addressed here. When the central focus of biblical worship is established, it points in all aspects to Jesus Christ as Lord and God at work through Christ's birth, death and resurrection. According to Gerhard Delling, the well-known New Testament scholar, 'it is no longer God who "builds" this Church, but Jesus. That corresponds exactly to the way in which Jesus elsewhere took statements made in the Old Testament about God and applied them to Himself. He is the One who not only carries out the commission of God but in whom God Himself acts' (1962: 19–20). The Old Testament continually points toward the life and work of the coming Christ; the New Testament presents the story of his birth, his ministry, and ultimately his death and resurrection and then shows how the different authors and early believers worked out their theology based on Jesus Christ as Lord. Worship of the God of the Old Testament points to Christ; worship of the living Christ of the New Testament points back to God. The Holy Spirit, given as the ongoing substitute for Christ's physical presence (John 16:7), also continually directs attention towards him.

Having this understanding of the centrality of Jesus Christ as the key to biblical worship helps to put some things in perspective. There will always be debate about worship, but however the term is used, and regardless of how broad or narrow the use, if it is to be biblical, Christ must be central. If 'worship' is used in the context of worship service, worship team, worship leader, the bottom line in determining the role and the validity of that role must be the centrality of Christ. Herzog rightly states: 'Unmistakably Christian worship points to Jesus of Nazareth' (1973: 133). Although it would be far too simple to say that this focus eliminates the problems faced in contemporary worship and the differing understandings and practical expressions of it, it does however set a biblical framework and a standard by which to evaluate, a criterion for assessment of some of the things which may uncritically be called worship.

With this mark of Christ-centredness as the standard of biblical worship, Christ-centredness should be evident in the various practical expressions of worship. In contemporary Christian worship, perhaps no area consistently arouses more controversy than music. Nevertheless, without prejudging the specific kinds of music that are to be encouraged in the Church, there are some biblical precepts that emerge, and they are surprisingly consistent with the pattern of Christ-centredness established above.

Although there is little idea what the music of the Old or New Testaments would have sounded like, it can be seen that it was an important part of the worship of the Church. Some of the terms in the New Testament for the music of the believers are 'psalms, hymns, and spiritual songs' (Eph. 5:19; Col. 3:16).[1] Without knowing exactly what these may have referred to in the early Church, it is quite certain that they at least indicate that music was a vital part of their gatherings.

When it comes to establishing the content of early Christian music many scholars look to several New Testament prayers that may well have been early Christian hymns. There is a noticeable consistency in their focus. Luke 1:46–55, Mary's song, *praises God for the Son* she would soon bear; later in the same chapter (vv. 68–79), Zechariah's song *praises God* for the fulfillment of his promises to his people, a God who would *through Christ* 'give his people the knowledge of salvation through the forgiveness of their sins' (v. 77). In Luke 2:29–32 Simeon *praises God for Jesus*, the salvation for the people. Philippians 2:6–11, probably the most important early Christian confession, powerfully *depicts Christ*, obedient

[1]Biblical quotations are from the New International Version.

to death on a cross, but exalted to the highest place, 'that at the name of Jesus every knee should bow ... and every tongue *confess that Jesus Christ is Lord* ...' (vv. 10, 11). Finally, Colossians 1:15–20 vividly *describes Jesus* as pre-eminently 'the head of the body, the church'. These examples 'can legitimately be seen as reflecting the sort of liturgical material which early Christians would have used' (Bradshaw 1992: 44). Regardless of the sound or style of these songs, if indeed they were songs, there is one evident pattern – they all have Christ as their central focus. By now the pattern should be evident that early Christian worship focused upon Christ, as the pertinent biblical texts clearly reveal. This may come as a surprise to some, who are accustomed to separating emotional from cerebral elements in worship. The fact that the music of the early Church had a clear focus upon Christ indicates that worship requires an engagement of both heart *and* mind with God. As Paul says in 1 Corinthians 14:13b, 14, 'For if I pray in a tongue, my spirit prays, but my mind is unfruitful. So what shall I do? I will pray with my spirit, but I will also pray with my mind; I will sing with my spirit, but I will also sing with my mind'. It is crucial that this quality be present for worship to become more than simply empty words, motions, or emotions.

Elements of biblical worship are not restricted to the church-gathering but can and should become an integral part of everyday life to really become the worship portrayed in the New Testament. 'All Christian life is worship, "liturgy" means service, all believers share Christ's priesthood, and the whole Christian Church is the house of God (1 Cor. 3:16, Eph. 2:22)' (Moule 1961: 84). However, for the subject at hand the practice as it takes place in formal church gatherings will be considered.

What the Liturgy and Worship of a Church Indicate

The above discussion may seem rather academic. In a sense it is, except that it is important to note that ideas motivate practice. As John Barkley comments,

> we see how doctrine or dogma determines worship. The character of worship springs from the nature and character of the God who is believed in. Our concept of God and the way we manifest and expound his relation to man determine our worship ... just as theology influences liturgy, so liturgy influences theology, because it brings theological statements before the bar of experience. (1973: 7)

Thus, the order of a church service, the time given to various elements of it, elements included or excluded all serve as indicators of the priorities of a particular church. From these it can be seen which things are considered important, and which are not. 'In many respects the essence of a religion is more directly intelligible in its worship than in statements of its basic principles or even in descriptions of its sentiments' (Delling 1962: xi). Therefore, it is worthwhile to note some of the contrasts of various churches and identify what may be indicated by a single element: a church which emphasises mostly the spontaneous expressions of individuals compared with a church which keeps to a written congregational response; one where a priest's role is highly revered compared with one that subscribes only to the 'priesthood' of the believers; the use of formal individual hymns at various times in the service compared with twenty to thirty minutes of sustained singing of contemporary songs; the antiquity of an order of service contrasted with the recent copyright dates of all materials used in a service; exuberant clapping and dancing in one church building contrasted with a hushed silence in another; the use of the creeds compared with the ever-changing 'word of knowledge'; the formal written-out prayer in one, the extemporaneous prayer in another, etc. Without making judgements on any of these particular items, it can be agreed that the actual practices illustrate something of the nature or focus of a given church. By taking a closer look at the way these elements of corporate worship are all worked together in a church, however, some definite assessments can be made of the priorities and character of that church. If the practices of individual churches carry out the beliefs and practices of a movement, then it is possible by logical extension to make some valid statements about the movement as well.

What becomes increasingly apparent is that the manner of worship and the patterns of a particular group may point quite clearly in directions that are not at all what that group had intended or realised. Here some disturbing things emerge about the nature of the worship that is taking place in the churches that are involved in the current phenomena of the Toronto Blessing. In taking up the concept of worship, looking at it from several angles in the light of the churches participating in the Toronto Blessing and against the background of their biblical roots and traditions, it is possible to draw some conclusions and indicate some signs that should perhaps be heeded.

Specific Historical Church Models and their Practices

Churches have historically had various ways of coming to terms with the biblical concept of the Christ-centredness of worship. Not everyone is agreed that the historical practices of a church are to be kept at all costs, nor that they necessarily continue to signify biblical precepts and practices. However, it seems that history must be acknowledged as a major participant in the discussion, based on the fact that Christians for generations have debated similar kinds of issues. Practices that have been preserved may have more to say than present generations would like to admit. Looking very briefly at four models of churches, all claiming to be trying to maintain significant features of New Testament practice and Christian history, will provide necessary background. The categories used are not ironclad, since there are numerous churches that emphasise more than one of the models below. But the characterisations can be useful for instructive purposes.

BAPTIST – BAPTISM

In baptist churches, as is evident by the name, one of the central focuses is upon water baptism, usually defined as believer's baptism. There are numerous examples and commands in the New Testament that give credence to the biblical basis of this practice and hence the legitimacy of its occupying a central place in the worship of churches persuaded by these examples (e.g. Matt. 28:16–20 especially v. 19; John 3:22, 23; Acts 2:38, 41; 8:38; 12:30, 31; 10:48; 16:31–33). The examples are all of new believers being obedient to the command to believe or repent and be baptised, and, as a result, going through some sort of water baptism as an integral part of their belief in Christ. Without debating the modes of baptism at this point, it can be seen that the New Testament gives substantial background and basis for the practice observed by baptists. For many of these churches, baptism occupies a special place in worship services, or may even constitute a separate service dedicated to the practice.

CHARISMATIC – TONGUES

Charismatic churches, including Pentecostals, along with various denominations which may be considered charismatic, believe that there are certain signs of being filled with the Holy Spirit, having received a second work of the Spirit or being baptised in the Spirit. These signs have traditionally been evidenced by the gift of speaking in tongues and secondarily by the gift of interpretation of tongues. Other gifts of the Spirit have also been highlighted, but these two are the distinctive ones. There are numerous references to both the practice and problems of speaking in tongues and interpretation of tongues in the early Church (e.g. 1 Cor. 12—14, Acts 2:4, 15). It is interesting to note that Peter used the presence of the phenomena as a way of pointing people to Jesus of Nazareth and presenting his story (Acts 2:22–24). Regardless of the other issues that this issue raises, it is enough at this point to note that tongues were a genuine part of the New Testament accounts of at least some early Christian churches. The manifestation of the charismatic gifts, including especially the gift of tongues, has continued to occupy a significant place in various charismatic worship services. This can be seen in times devoted to speaking or singing in tongues, either individually or as a corporate exercise.

EVANGELICAL – THE PREACHED WORD

For many years, in the typical Evangelical Protestant church, the preacher's sermon, or exposition of the word and proclamation of the Gospel, has been considered the core of the service, with other elements pointing towards it and generally seen as less important. This stems from a belief in the word of God as foundational to one's faith, and therefore necessarily preached and taught for the people to learn from and to obey (2 Tim. 3:16). For example, in Luke 4:15–30, Jesus reads from Isaiah 61:1–2 and proclaims the day of the Lord to be at hand. In Paul's numerous trips to the synagogue, it says that he showed how Christ had fulfilled the Old Testament Scriptures. Biblical proclamation has continued to occupy a place of prime importance in numerous churches. Of course, the sermon has gone through an evolution in recent years and in many cases has become less substantive and more superficial, speaking to the felt needs of the moment, but not necessarily to the long-term needs of the listener. Nevertheless, the sermon's importance continues.

SACRAMENTAL — EUCHARIST

In sacramentalist churches, including such churches as the Anglican, the Eucharist is the focal point. As a near-weekly observance it is not difficult to pinpoint the central role it plays in the worship and liturgy. The death and resurrection of Christ are pivotal to the entire New Testament and therefore crucial for the worship priorities of sacramental churches. The biblical and historical precedents for this practice are substantial. During the last supper with the disciples, Jesus broke bread, representing his body, and offered the cup as his 'blood of the covenant, which is poured out for many for the forgiveness of sins' (Matt. 26:26–28). In 1 Corinthians 11:26, following the account of the last supper, it says 'proclaim the Lord's death until he comes'. Just as these were important in the early Church, so they have traditionally been significant parts of much Christian worship. It is not necessary to observe many sacramental services to realise that the Eucharist is often half the time of any given service, and placed as the latter half to give predominance to it. The formal liturgy moves unhesitatingly towards the celebration of the Eucharist and culminates in it.

SUMMARY OF THE CHURCHES

As with any church or denomination, practices are adapted with time and boundaries between denominations become somewhat blurred or changed, but it can be agreed, I think, that each of the four church orientations above represents a distinctive set of church practices endorsed by biblical precedent and agreed upon by previous generations of Christians of each denominational type as central to their theology and their worship. Each distinctive practice is focused in some significant way on Jesus Christ. Each has a biblical basis and early Church practice as its foundation, as well as a long line of historical tradition to give credence to it. Finally, each is normally evident by its prominence in the service in the individual church.

Observation and Assessment of Contemporary Practices in Churches Experiencing the Toronto Blessing

Introduction

There are probably few churches of any description that could stand up to objective scrutiny without revealing some inadequacy or some failure to keep priorities, order and balance. Nonetheless, the purpose here is to determine the nature of the worship that is taking place specifically in the Toronto Blessing churches by observing some of their practices and measuring them against the standards described earlier as the basis for determining biblical worship. This exercise could certainly be used not only in churches that are experiencing the Toronto Blessing, but also in any church willing to take stock of what its worship services may suggest compared with what its own perceptions, ideals or official statements may indicate.

Vineyard Roots of the Toronto Blessing

One thing that seems to be consistent in this movement of the Toronto Blessing is that it has strong ties to the Vineyard movement, with the phenomenon of the Blessing said to be stemming from an outbreaking of the Spirit at the Toronto Airport Vineyard in Toronto, Canada. Churches participating in this experience of the Blessing have not necessarily been connected with the Vineyard previously, but have come into contact as a result.

One feature of the Vineyard movement has been the way its leaders have picked up on the genuine desire of many individuals to have a more personal element in their worship services. The leaders have been creative and diligent in disseminating their teachings, music and various other materials reflecting this desire for personal worship, both to those within the movement and also to others who are interested. But it appears that individuals and churches who have not aligned themselves previously with the Vineyard may have proceeded to buy a product of the Vineyard without necessarily investigating the background or potential outcome of it. Perhaps without consciously accepting the theology and practices of the Vineyard movement, many have adopted them without realising it. There is legitimate debate about some of these, and regardless of where a person may end up at the end of the discussion, it seems important at least to know the issues. Two such issues can make the point adequately. The first concerns the fact that many of the churches displaying the Toronto Blessing are aligning themselves with a movement that has had trouble with establishing the validity of its so-called prophets' messages. The second issue is that of an open canon, that is, that God's revelation extends beyond the confines of the revelation of the Bible. The issue of the open canon is one that not all Christians, perhaps not even all members of the Vineyard, would be willing to accept. If the biblical canon is still open for additions (and deletions?) and any individual can be a receiver of additional revelations, this raises the serious question of who then determines which things are really biblical. Yet this openness is apparently an underlying foundation of the theology of the Vineyard. For this present study and its analysis of biblical worship, in order to agree upon a basis for what constitutes biblical worship, 'biblical' must remain that which is already in the written Bible, with tradition, historical factors and contemporary society definitely coming into play but not accepted as constituting that which is biblical.

Several churches in Britain that are experiencing the Blessing have apparently flown individuals to Toronto to learn more about the phenomenon, evidently gathering biblical texts to provide their bases, learning techniques of administering or facilitating the Blessing and generally gaining more experience of the Blessing themselves (see Dixon 1994: passim). One woman described her experience of being in a room full of pastors or ministers who, during a time of the Blessing, began to make various loud noises, many of them 'animal–like'. She also felt herself about to 'roar' and, in fact, did 'roar'. But, simply because there are many pastors or ministers present does not in itself make something biblical, so this cannot count as evidence in the search for the signs of biblical worship. Another factor which cannot be used as evidence of something being biblical is that of the success of some churches, either in their use of a particular technique or in the manifestation of some fascinating phenomena. Success of these kinds cannot serve as a criterion for what is biblical.

Others, with great enthusiasm, are flying to various countries to teach churches how to experience the Blessing in their own churches where it has not already reached them. It appears that for some, simply duplicating the effect of the Blessing is primary, rather than actually knowing its biblical basis or status. The Blessing may indeed be all that everyone experiencing it hopes it is, but so far, few who have defended it have been able to articulate their defence clearly and scripturally. While one would not want to miss the outpouring of the Holy Spirit purely on academic grounds, equally it would seem foolish to ignore the evidence if it does end up pointing in some other direction.

Elements of Worship in the Churches of the Toronto Blessing

In the light of what has been said above, and using the discussion above as a model, it is important now to describe and evaluate the actual practices of Toronto Blessing churches. The following picture emerges from having read many descriptions of the worship services and having attended a number of different kinds of services. I cannot claim to have anything representing a complete picture, but several patterns have nevertheless emerged. Before describing those practices that were evidenced, it is worth noting that in the services observed there was no use of the Lord's Prayer, no recited creed of any sort, no celebration of the Eucharist, no singing of hymns, and little reading of the Bible. This does not indicate that they are never included in these various churches, but it is a point of interest.

Tongues were used, but never just two or three people speaking in tongues in orderly fashion, and there was no interpretation (1 Cor. 14:27–28). 'Words of knowledge' and 'prophecy' were terms used in some services, with individuals using these as a means of speaking words of encouragement to other individuals or the group as a whole. These will not be dwelt upon, however, since they are part of more wide-spread charismatic phenomena and did not appear to be used in a way that highly influenced the manifestation of the Toronto Blessing.

MUSIC

Although music was discussed above in terms of its biblical foundations, it is now appropriate to apply what was said to the use of music in Toronto Blessing churches. The musicians in the various services observed were of varying calibre and proficiency, but the style of music and its presentation were similar, using the worship band or team. The model was that of an individual song or worship leader, several vocalists, and a small ensemble of instrumentalists, generally including piano or electronic keyboard, guitar, bass, electric guitar, drums, and one or two other instruments. The singing was not exceptional in any case, neither in the leader, the assisting vocalists, nor in the congregation, but some was noticeably better than others.

The actual songs in every case observed were contemporary. In at least 90 per cent of the songs used where copyright information was included and presented legibly, the copyright dates were from the last two years. None of the services included anything that could be mistaken for a hymn, although one incorporated a contemporary setting to words of a prayer from the Anglican Alternative Service Book. The majority of the songs referred to personal needs and were addressed to the Spirit or were requests of God for 'more' of the Spirit.

Perhaps one of the main underlying causes of the wide-spread movement towards the use of worship teams in contemporary churches is reaction to old models of church which have seemed to become impersonal and irrelevant for present-day people and culture. Part of the effort of those working towards both the implementation of newer songs and the concept of the worship team, therefore, has been to personalise the worship service. Many contemporary songs are written in the first person, with a strong sense of personal and intimate relationship with God, and the worship team, though a group in appearance, is often very individualistic in nature. However, in evaluating the songs in terms of the biblical criteria listed above, something is lost in utilising only contemporary songs which tend to focus on 'me' and 'how I feel about God', and the worship team without careful direction sometimes fosters a contrived individuality that often accompanies a stage performance and draws more attention to itself. There seems to be a lack of responsibility and maturity evident in some of these groups, or on the part of their leader. Another problem that current worship groups tend to bring to the forefront is an insatiable need for 'new' and 'contemporary' without a bridge to the traditional teaching and historical practices of that church. Of course, simply because something has been done for dozens or hundreds of years doesn't make it good, but one must wonder whether those making decisions about music and other elements of a worship service are aware of the implications of their practices, especially those that seem to show a disregard of biblical and historical precedent. In general, comparing the lyrics and melodies of these songs with others of the same genre, most were not, in my opinion, of exceptional quality or musicality – they were not songs that I would expect still to hear in a year or two. More importantly, few if any of the songs were about Christ or things foundational to the Christian faith; the songs were consistently about 'me' as an individual, and were apparently used to focus the individual on furthering the effects of the Blessing.

Prayer

The use of prayer merits similar evaluation. The prayers were sometimes focused on aspects of the current phenomena, calling on God to bring 'more, more'; at other times the prayers were addressed to the Spirit and focused on a particular individual, apparently with the goal of that person falling to the floor. These prayers appeared to become quite urgent and repetitive, even forced, when the individual did not fall quickly or at all. Various people were called up at different times to be prayed for or to participate in the praying. In one instance, several who were visiting to learn about the phenomena but who were not known by name were invited up in the morning service to be prayed for but were the ones asked to do the praying in the evening service. Apparently their experience of the Blessing in the morning qualified them to administer it in the evening. It appeared that, as with the songs, the Blessing or some manifestation of the Spirit was usually the actual focus of the prayers, rather than God and his work through Christ.

Sermon

The sermon or talk continues to be used in Toronto Blessing churches. At one church, one short message was used as a means of establishing the validity of the Toronto Blessing. There was no actual evidence given from the Bible apart from single verses taken at random and an Old Testament story used as a contemporary allegory of the Toronto Blessing, accompanied by numerous warnings to those who may be sceptical about the Blessing. This evidently was to set the stage for what was to follow, which was a testimony about the Blessing and then the 'ministry time'. In another church, the message was directed to the people of that church, addressing an issue that had seemed to become pertinent in their church regarding the Blessing. It appears that sermons, rather than being concerned to deepen the biblical or spiritual understanding of the congregation, are often being used apologetically to substantiate and reinforce credibility for the Blessing.

TESTIMONIES

Testimonies, long a staple of more informal and often evangelical churches, continue to be used in Toronto Blessing churches. In several of the services, personal testimonies were given about the experience of the Blessing or something related, and were used as preparation for the 'ministry time' which followed. Some testimonies were also used as an opportunity to pray for the person who had given the testimony, with the intent of allowing that person to fall publicly under the power of the Spirit or the Blessing, but with no mention of Jesus. Apparently this practice of praying for the person who has just testified is recommended in Vineyard materials (Dixon 1994: 325).

MINISTRY TIME

'Ministry time' is the term that is used to describe the dedicated time in the service when the manifestations of the Spirit are expected to be present. Typically during ministry time, attenders were instructed to stack their chairs around the edges of the room. In one service, no one could remain seated for this time unless they made their way through the crowd to the balcony. This ministry time was not a case of individuals coming forward for prayer or taking the initiative in order to receive some sort of ministry or experience of the Blessing; instead it was an experience *en masse*. For someone who may not have been prepared for the experience, it required actively moving away from the crowd. Immediately people were groaning, lying on the floor, laughing, flapping their hands and arms, making indiscernible noises which may have been animal-like, while others were more orgiastic in nature. Some were shaking violently, others were weeping. Some discreetly looked around them after a time and then began their particular noise or action again. Ministry team members – apparently those who have experienced the Blessing's outward manifestations – actively moved from person to person, raising a hand above the individual's forehead or behind their back and apparently praying for or speaking with them, clearing things from behind the person before the person fell, or actually helping them on to the floor. The fact that everything began on cue poses some difficulties, although further reports indicate that where the church leader has led the way in allowing these signs earlier in the service, the eruptions have become more frequent at different times throughout a service. Other churches have begun including the ministry time in various sections of the service, as well as having a more concentrated time at one particular point, usually near the end of the service. However, it also appears that the Blessing can be timed, planned, re-enacted whenever it is wanted or needed, whether it be a morning, evening, second service, or the like.

In one service, throughout the ministry time, the pastor kept control of the environment by repeatedly speaking to those who were not evidencing outward signs and reiterating that this was acceptable and not to worry, praying at times, directing ministry team members to other individuals, calling for more members to help, and eventually closing the service down. In another, the pastor continually gave signs to the people, by his actions and personal responses to what was going on in the general part of the service, indicating that responding throughout the service in the varying ways of the Blessing was acceptable, even desirable. At no point was there any specific mention of Christ, no direction given for the person who wanted to know about Christ, and no Gospel preached. It appeared in each case that as far as the pastor was concerned, the obvious manifestations of the Spirit or the Blessing (and apparently these are being equated) were the central issue. And it seems to be assumed that whatever state one gets into during the ministry time is 'of God'.

Perhaps something that would be worth considering for a moment is if indeed God did not choose to act in a particular ministry time, if the Holy Spirit did not come upon anyone at the specific time, would anyone notice? Or would the phenomena still be present? Would it simply be a case of the 'show must go on', and the ministry time would continue as usual?

The above description gives a brief evaluation of the major features of a typical Toronto Blessing worship service. From the criteria established above, their relation to the Christ-centredness of Christian worship has been mentioned. This effort has been characterised by evaluation in terms of what the Blessing churches themselves do. But it seems important that their overall pattern of worship must also be evaluated in terms of the major models of church worship as well.

Four Church Models for Comparison

Although the Toronto Blessing churches are distinguished by their common manifestations of the phenomena of the Blessing in their worship services, these churches have much longer-standing ties to the traditional models briefly discussed above. When these general patterns of worship are compared with what is taking place in the Toronto Blessing churches some noteworthy patterns emerge, including some significant changes of focus. It is perhaps worthwhile to note these, if for no other reason than many connected with the

Blessing may not be aware of the implications of the shifts in emphasis.

BAPTIST

What seems to have become dominant in baptist churches that are now experiencing the Toronto Blessing is not that people are coming to Christ and being baptised, as one might expect, but that believers are coming for the Blessing or 'ministry time'. In one church, other church members come from neighbouring churches to participate, not in the service but only in the ministry time. While this may be beneficial in some respects, the question must be raised: has the Blessing or ministry time become more important than people coming to faith and being baptised, even though baptism is a central focus in the New Testament and one woven throughout the tradition and theology of the baptistic churches? While it is admirable that one pastor admitted that ironically people are not coming to Christ and being baptised, and urged his people *not* to forget baptism and *not* to let the ministry time become focal in their minds, it seemed evident that indeed that has been happening in at least one Baptist church experiencing the Blessing.

CHARISMATIC

In the charismatic tradition, where tongues is the evidence of being Spirit-filled, the Toronto Blessing can be seen usurping the place of tongues and becoming the new evidence of the Spirit's work. Whether one agrees or not with the basis for tongues as the sign of being Spirit-filled, a sudden change of signs does raise questions. In the words of one well-known charismatic theologian, Clifford Hill, 'loud, uncontrollable, hysterical laughter has no precedent in scripture as a manifestation of the Spirit of God' (September/October 1994: 10). The Toronto Blessing is a recent phenomenon with far less biblical basis to substantiate it than tongues, yet charismatics have been quick to accept it as a new sign. If charismatics are concerned about the biblical and historical basis for their practices and beliefs, then this element of their worship must also fall under scrutiny.

EVANGELICAL

In churches with a heritage of the word or Gospel message being predominant, the Blessing seems to have upstaged the message and become the climax of the service. The message is used as a means of asserting that the Blessing is valid or as a time for talking about the Blessing, but not apparently as a time to present the claims of Christ. This replacement of one main emphasis for another needs to be questioned. This is not simply a case of exchanging one hymn for a contemporary chorus, nor of adjusting the order of the service; this is substituting a major historical emphasis on teaching or preaching the Bible – a cognitive dimension of the Christian life – for a completely different emphasis: one on outward emotive manifestations.

SACRAMENTAL

In looking at a sacramental liturgical model, such as the Anglican, in terms of the Toronto Blessing, another major substitution has occurred. The corporate breaking of the bread and the sharing of the cup has been a traditional link to the biblical account of the Last Supper, instituting the bread and wine as remembrances of Jesus' death and resurrection and the forgiveness of sins available as a result. In sacramental churches, the Blessing has apparently superceded the Eucharist as the high point and focus of liturgical practice. Warner makes the enthusiastic comment regarding the presence of the Blessing that on one occasion 'So overwhelming was the response that a planned communion service had to be cancelled' (1995: 16). The remembrance of Christ's death and resurrection, the observance of them certainly at the heart of the sacramental liturgy, has been, if not literally removed from the liturgy, certainly replaced in importance.

SUMMARY OF THE FOUR CHURCHES

Perhaps these substitutions have only occurred in those churches where their traditional focus no longer has meaning for the people. If this is the case, then several questions should be raised. When there is an emptiness in worship, might it not be easier to begin to worship an ephemeral experience that feels good or temporarily appeases, rather than worshipping the risen Christ as Lord? Does the Blessing fill in wherever there is a void of some sort in the liturgy? If so, shouldn't it be investigated thoroughly before being accepted? Since many Toronto Blessing churches claim to be 'word and spirit' churches, shouldn't they be searching the Bible at least as diligently as they seek the manifestations of the Spirit? Shouldn't they consult biblical beliefs and historical practices of the church thoroughly before discarding what has been the heart of their Christian worship? The solution to empty worship might well be to return to the traditional biblical and historical basis of worship rather than abandoning it for a spectacular current phenomenon.

General Evaluation

Loss of Traditional Focus of Worship

Living in a day and age when traditional values are suspect, historical ways of doing things are discarded as *passé*, family ties are increasingly broken and rewoven into different patterns, and more and more products on the market are instantly gratifying and constantly changing shape and colour, it is perhaps not surprising to find the Church also trying to establish new ways of doing things and looking for more exciting and fascinating elements to liven up worship services and make them relevant and to address the countless needs of the contemporary individual and family. But in the craze to find new and exciting elements, or in getting caught up in the latest thing, churches run the greatest risk of losing what is of proven worth and value. Each of the kinds of churches mentioned above – baptistic, charismatic, evangelical and sacramental – stands to lose a significant element of the traditional focus of its worship under the influence of the Toronto Blessing. These churches may, consciously or unconsciously, be trading in a traditional focus for one that has little biblical basis, was not apparently endorsed by the practice of the early Church, and may very well be short-lived. Horn makes some insightful comments regarding the phenomena recorded in the opening chapters of Acts: 'How did the apostles react to these occurrences? Did they . . . dwell on them or seek to reproduce them?' He shows what Peter's response was:

> What he did was to move rapidly from the external signs to the essential message. From bewildering events to the truths that made clear his hearers' relation to God. From what they saw to what they needed to hear. In other words, he wanted them to listen to the truths about how they stood before God, about their guilt for the crucifixion, about the rising and exaltation of Jesus, about their need to repent and be baptised. (Horn February/March 1995)

Perhaps Peter's example of holding on to his original purpose, regardless of events that could easily have diverted him or even have been exploited, is the example most needed in relation to the Toronto Blessing.

Loss of Christ-Centred Worship

Although the phenomena of the Toronto Blessing are spreading from church to church, city to city, and from one continent to another, and while the enthusiasm of church leaders steadily mounts and more and more individuals personally experience the Blessing, the foundations for it in Christ-centred worship remain weak and insubstantial. It is important to remember that this discussion is not about whether or not these phenomena exist; the question is whether the current patterns of worship retain their 'Christian' focus. What has been seen so far in the Blessing churches is the phenomena being given top priority, while significant biblical elements of worship are being cast aside, treated as less important or even used as a vehicle to promote the Blessing. Perhaps Colossians 3:16–17 speaks to the point:

> Let the word of Christ dwell in you richly as you teach and admonish one another with all wisdom, and as you sing psalms, hymns and spiritual songs with gratitude in your hearts to God. And whatever you do, whether in word or deed, do it all in the name of the Lord Jesus, giving thanks to God the Father through him.

It seems that Paul has indeed captured the appropriate balance regarding Christian worship in the blending of teaching and instruction, music and praise, all in the name of the Lord Jesus, with thanks to God.

Self-Centred Worship of the Blessing

Bell says that 'Christian worship is never meant to be an end in itself, nor does it exist to simply meet our personal and selfish needs' (1993: 172). In the churches that are experiencing the Toronto Blessing, it seems that the Blessing has become an end in itself, satisfying personal needs. The focus appears to have shifted from God or Christ-centredness and has instead become preoccupied with self and its gratification. The Blessing has taken the place of things that have historically, biblically, and theologically been central and foundational to the Christian faith. The lyrics of the songs used are not about Jesus Christ, the message is not the redemptive message of Christ, testimonies are not typically about Jesus, the celebration of the Eucharist has been replaced by 'ministry time', people are not coming to Christ and being baptised, and the congregation is not talking about Jesus. In fact, the primary thing people seem to be talking about is the Blessing. In a generation of 'me'-centredness, in this instance many in the Church may have fallen prey to the very thing that the Church is meant to oppose, the exaltation of the individual over the exaltation of Christ. The Blessing or 'ministry time' has taken the central role in the services and is the drawing card for those who attend. If church attendance alone is the bottom line, then this may be acceptable; if biblical worship is more important, then it is unacceptable. In looking at the actual practices of these churches, the visible evidence seems to indicate that the Blessing itself and its effect on the individual has become the thing worshipped. If nothing else, perhaps this brief analysis of worship associated with the Toronto Blessing will encourage churches or individuals to look at their own beliefs and check their practices against what they say that they believe. There is no question that there is something missing in many churches, that many have lost their vitality and the form of worship has become so dominating in some that it has practically eliminated the expressive life of the Church. But perhaps in addressing this need something else is lost. The Toronto Blessing churches have adopted a very informal nature, perhaps as a reaction to the old models of church which have emphasised form over expression. Peterson says something worth considering on this point, addressing both sides of the issue: 'Formality may be the expression of a very narrow and inadequate view of worship and informality may be an excuse for lack of preparation or any serious attempt to engage collectively with God' (1992: 160). Perhaps there is a need to look for something less sensational and more substantial in worship. One's emotions may easily be drawn to worship the Toronto Blessing, but it requires determination of the mind and heart to worship the risen Christ. The story of Jesus may be very old, but it becomes new in the retelling and living of it. Regardless of how a person *feels* about worship (and the Bible has very little to say about one's feelings about worship), in order to worship in a biblical sense, the Lordship of Christ must be pre-eminent, and it requires the mind as well as the heart to be actively participating.

Bibliography

Barkley, J. M. (1973) 'The Theology of Liturgy', *Liturgical Review 3*, no. 1, 1–15.

Bell, J. L. (1993) *Bridge over Troubled Water: ministry to baby boomers – a generation adrift*, Wheaton, IL: Victor Books.

Bradshaw, P. F. (1992) *The Search for the Origins of Christian Worship: sources and methods for the study of early liturgy*, London: SPCK.

Delling, D. G. (1962) *Worship in the New Testament*, translated by P. Scott, London: Darton, Longman and Todd.

Dixon, P. (1994) *Signs of Revival*, Eastbourne: Kingsway.

Herzog, F. (1973) 'The Norm and Freedom of Christian Worship', in M. H. Shepherd, Jr (ed.), *Worship in Scripture and Tradition*, New York: Oxford University Press, 98–133.

Hill, C. (September/October 1994) ' "Toronto Blessing" – True or False?' *Prophecy Today 10*, no. 2, 10–13.

Horn, B. (February/March 1995) 'Some Reflections on the Toronto Blessing', *NB*, Leicester: Universities and Colleges Christian Fellowship.

Moule, C. F. D. (1961) *Worship in the New Testament*, London: Lutterworth Press.

Peterson, D. (1992) *Engaging with God: a biblical theology of worship*, Grand Rapids: Eerdmans.

Warner, R. (1995) *Prepare for Revival*, London: Hodder and Stoughton.